HEARD ANY
GOOD ONES LATELY?

"Many people feel that one must have some extraordinary ability in order to remember and tell jokes, but that's not true! With a little coaching, anyone can be a great joke teller, and it's never too late to start. Everyone likes to be able to make people laugh and *anyone* can do it! Short and tall, husky and trim, rich and poor, young and old, *everyone* has the ability to create hilarity. Telling jokes is *most definitely* an equal opportunity employer!"

JIM PIETSCH

WHICH REMINDS ME OF THE
ONE ABOUT THE QUEEN OF
ENGLAND AND THE DUCK . . .

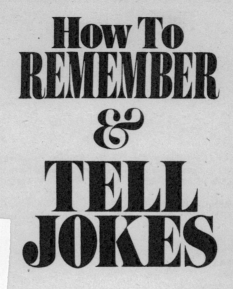

How To REMEMBER & TELL JOKES

WRITTEN AND ILLUSTRATED BY

JIM PIETSCH

AVON BOOKS  NEW YORK

Excerpts from *Using Humor for Effective Business Speaking* by Gene Perret, © 1989 by Gene Perret, reprinted by permission of Sterling Publishing Co., Inc., 387 Park Avenue South, New York, New York 10016.

HOW TO REMEMBER & TELL JOKES is an original publication of Avon Books. This work has never before appeared in book form.

AVON BOOKS
A division of
The Hearst Corporation
1350 Avenue of the Americas
New York, New York 10019

Text and illustrations copyright © 1992 by Jim Pietsch
Published by arrangement with the author
Library of Congress Catalog Card Number: 91-93027
ISBN: 0-380-76494-6

First Avon Books Printing: April 1992

AVON TRADEMARK REG. U.S. PAT. OFF. AND IN OTHER COUNTRIES, MARCA REGISTRADA. HECHO EN U.S.A.

Printed in the U.S.A.

RA 10 9 8 7 6 5 4 3 2 1

This book is dedicated to
PATTI BREITMAN
—always my champion

Contents

ACKNOWLEDGMENTS

First of all, I would like to thank my network of joke tellers who have given me such an abundant supply of laughter and friendship: Frank and Christine Baier, Jim Block, Donald Burton, Didi Conn, Jake Ehrenreich, Harry Ettling, Eric Frandsen, Laurie Kuslansky, Daniel Neiden, Tom and Jane Pandalakis, Marty Sheller, Carl Woitach, Sarah Zahn, and especially Johnny "Ethan" Phillips.

I would also like to thank my friends who have given me so much love and support: Jack Bashkow, Greg Fensterman, Len Freas, Michele Gani, Doug Hall, T. J. Johnson, Roy Miller, George Paris, Paul and Anita Pride, Eddie "Gua Gua" Rivera and Kathy, Joanne Regan, David Robb, Patti Sietz, Mark and Edie Worthy, and Bob "The Walking Encyclopedia" Waldman.

My family continues to show me that laughter makes life worth living: Barb and Berk Adams, Bill and Weezie Pietsch, Patti, Mark, Shauna and Alea Wise, and Barb Shultz. Thank you all for your laughter, love, and unwavering support.

Thanks go to my typists: Marian Kirchwehm, René Diggles, and especially Elise Morris. Thank you also to Gary and Gean Giambalvo from Studio G and Joe Grysko.

Special thanks go to Patti Bretiman, Laurie Kuslansky, Weezie Pietsch, and Karen Wexler for their ideas and opinions that helped shape the chapter "For Women Only."

My editor David Highfill has been a joy to work with and I thank him for his contributions and faith in my work.

Finally, I would like to thank Karen Wexler for her love and support throughout all phases of the extended process of writing this book. Her help went far beyond what I could ever have expected. She has shared with me her intelligence, talent, insight, sense of humor, and as an artist's assistant, she is the Zip-a-tone Queen. Baby, you're the greatest!

J. P.
N.Y.C.
1991

INTRODUCTION

If you are not able to remember or tell jokes, you are not alone.

While pursuing simultaneous careers in music, cartooning, and writing, I drove a taxicab part-time in New York City for five years. I have calculated that, in that period, I asked approximately twenty-five thousand people the same question: "Have you heard any good jokes lately?"

Much to my surprise, nine out of ten people—*ninety percent* of all my passengers—told me that they are unable to remember or tell jokes. Fortunately for me, the other ten percent were people like myself. If they could remember one joke they could remember a hundred, and they happily kept me in great supply.

Since I was hearing so many truly fantastic jokes, I decided to write a book and share my collection with everyone. My first book, *The New York City Cab Driver's Joke Book*, was published in 1986, and is still selling well.

But now I wonder why jokes, such great tools for fun and communication, should be told by only ten percent of the population. Many people think that one must have some extraordinary ability in order to remember and tell jokes, but that's not true. With a little coaching, *anyone* can be a great joke-teller, and it's never too late to start.

Because of my first book I have become a kind of joke magnet. People are always telling me jokes. Though by this time I've heard quite a few, I still enjoy them as much as I ever did. What I sense now, though, is just how powerful a good joke can be. When you share a laugh with someone, you connect in some way, and often feel an instant kinship.

Party-goers, public speakers, and businessmen have long recognized the power of making people laugh. Presidents of the United States have joke-writers working for them. This book is for anyone who wants to improve his or her ability to communicate, as well as for any person who just wants to be able to have some good laughs with friends.

Everyone loves jokes. I don't know anyone who says he doesn't want to hear a joke. On the contrary, many people say, "I could *use* hearing a good joke right now." Humor is a great release. It helps us to cope. A good laugh can help us see life from a different perspective and help us face our problems with renewed concentration and hope.

Even if you are one of those people who is able to remember and tell jokes, this book will help you to make your joke-telling more effective—and therefore funnier. It will also provide you with over one hundred great new jokes for your repertoire.

It has always been my belief that jokes are there to be shared and spread around. HAVE FUN!

CHAPTER 1

IT'S A JUNGLE OUT THERE

As you read these words, you are about to enter

This is a world inhabited by Martians and a talking koala bear, Moses and an electric guitarist, a little boy pretending to be a cowboy, a Japanese man with a wheelbarrow full of yen, a vulture and an airline stewardess, light bulbs, a pool table and a Rolls-Royce, and, of course, lots of laughing people. You can expect to find all of these delights and many, many more in the wonderful world of jokes.

Oscar Wilde said, "Laughter is not a bad beginning for a friendship." Indeed, laughter can help break the ice in many different situations. Parties, dates, business meetings, speeches, dinners, holiday gatherings, get-togethers with friends, and even cab rides—all become much more enjoyable with the shared laughter that a good joke can bring.

Right now, the world of joke-telling might seem rather frightening to you, full of pitfalls and hidden traps, ready to throw you into the muck and mire of rejection and humiliation.

Indeed, those dangers do exist in the world of jokes, just as a trip through the African jungle might hold the dangers of quicksand, poisonous plants, wild animals, and, no cable TV.

Because of this, you wouldn't think for a minute of taking a trip through the jungle all by yourself. If you did, it would be a terrifying struggle for survival—not the kind of journey that many of us, if given the choice, would choose to take.

However, a safari through the jungle with a qualified guide would be a completely different story. You could depend on your guide to show you through all the hazardous terrain and past the hidden dangers. You would also expect the guide to point out to you all the exotic plants and animals and to take you to many remote locations of natural splendor and beauty. This type of guided trip would be a very different experience from a solo excursion.

By plunking down your cash for this book, you have hereby bought my services to be your guide through the world of joke-telling. I will be your advisor, interpreter, navigator, protector, teacher, and, of course, jokester. I am here to show you the joys and wonders to be found in the world of joke-telling.

I will provide you with knowledge, understanding, and techniques you can use to help you remember and tell jokes. Once you have read this book, you will be able to find your own way through this fun-filled world of laughter and communication. You will have some great jokes in your repertoire and will be able to remember and tell them.

Before we embark on this journey, however, it is important that you understand that I am just like you. I am not a professional comedian. I am not like Robin Williams who can think up a funny line for every situation. I do not make up my jokes.

In this way, I am like the man who is widely considered to be the only U.S. president who was truly a humorist: Abraham Lincoln. About his jokes, Lincoln once said,

I REMEMBER A GOOD STORY WHEN I HEAR IT, BUT I NEVER INVENTED ANYTHING ORIGINAL. I AM ONLY A RETAIL DEALER.

As you can see from Honest Abe, it is not necessary to be able to make up jokes in order to enjoy telling them with great effectiveness.

Believe it or not, most people can tell jokes if they try hard enough. Nearly everyone has a joke-teller inside, waiting to be released out into the world. The fact that you are reading this now proves that you are one of those people.

If you didn't think it was possible for you to remember and tell jokes, you would have looked at the cover of this book and told yourself, ''Don't even bother.'' But you are reading this right now, which proves that even if you are skeptical, somewhere deep inside, you would like to be a better joke-teller.

Your Only Requirement Is DESIRE!

That, my friend, is the only character trait that you need in order to be a joke-teller: you just have to *want* to.

Being able to tell a joke and watching it create hilarity can be much more enjoyable than laughing at that joke in the first place. The look of satisfaction on a successful joke-teller's face is proof of that. Everyone likes to be able to make others laugh, and joke-telling is a skill that *can* be learned by *anyone*.

If you took a guided safari through the African jungle you would return home with many happy memories. There might have been some brushes with danger, but because of the skill of your guide, you were protected from any real peril and those moments only added thrills and excitement to your journey.

In much the same way, I will help to make your entry into the world of joke-telling as safe as possible. There will be *some* risks, of course, but they will be minimal, and the odds of survival are high. You will also feel the thrill of challenges met, barriers overcome.

By the end of this book, the jokester inside of you will bounce into your daily life whenever you need some fun. The laughter that you discover every time you hear and tell a "good one" will be your incentive to carry you through many years of sharing jokes with friends, colleagues, and people with whom you have nothing else in common.

Ready now?

CHAPTER 2

WHY SOME CAN TELL 'EM
AND SOME CAN'T

You know, I was discussing this unfortunate state of affairs with noted psychologist and joke-lover Dr. Lenny Bernstein. He proposed a theory to me that seemed to make a lot of sense.

> I THINK THAT WHETHER OR NOT YOU ARE A JOKE-TELLER TODAY PROBABLY HAS TO DO WITH YOUR VERY FIRST EXPERIENCE TELLING A JOKE.

For example, in your formative years, something like this might have happened to you: on a typical day in third grade you were standing on the playground with some friends before school. They were probably jump-roping, swing-setting, and teeter-tottering all around you. Then one of the boys in your group began to tell a joke.

> A REALLY SHY MAN, AND A REALLY SHY WOMAN GET MARRIED...†

YOU

*For complete joke, see page 151.

When he hit the end of the joke, you all started laughing. The punchline was a real surprise, was hilarious, and was even a little bit naughty, which made it all the funnier.

After school that day, you saw a group of kids that you had always wanted to know. Remembering what a big hit your friend was with his joke, you decided to go over and make a similar impression.

But it had been seven hours since you heard the joke—hours of math, science, and English. When you started to tell it, you realized that you couldn't quite remember it exactly as you had heard it.

Finally, you hit the punchline.

Not only did those other kids not laugh, but they walked away from you making cracks about the dangers of inbreeding. It would be another two years before they even spoke to you again.

And now you have carried this scar with you all your life.

However, *this* could have happened to you:

Instead of waiting all day to tell the joke to someone else, you ran into a friend just as you were walking into the building for your first class.

Since you had heard it only two minutes before, you remembered the joke perfectly, even down to the inflections, expressions, and hand gestures your friend had made when he told it.

When you hit the punchline, Joey laughed as hard as you did when you originally heard the joke.

You went on to tell the joke again to another friend during recess, again at lunch, and to another friend after school. Each time you told the joke, you got more and more into it, and you kept getting bigger and bigger laughs from your friends.

When you got home from school, you told the joke to your mom and dad. By now you had gotten to be an expert at telling it, and they laughed really hard.

THAT'S CUTE!

GOOD ONE!

AS A MATTER OF FACT, SON, I HAVE ONE FOR YOU! ONE DAY, A SECOND GRADE TEACHER ASKS HER CLASS...*

Your dad told you a really funny joke in return and you couldn't wait to get to school the next day to tell it to everybody. The following morning, just before you left, you asked your father to tell it to you one more time, just to refresh your memory.

As you walked to school, you repeated the joke over and over to yourself, making sure that you

*For complete joke, see page 163.

didn't forget anything. When you got there, you told your regular gang before classes started, and your other friends during recess and lunch.

They all liked the joke so much that after school you decided to try telling it to that other group of kids. They laughed the hardest of anybody, and, as a result, they became new friends.

You were now well on your way toward a lifetime as a GREAT JOKE-TELLER!

On the other hand, a third scenario could have gone like this. You heard the joke before school.

YOU ONCE MORE

Then you told it to other friends before school, at lunch, during recess, and after school, and got big laughs every time.

Then you hurried home to tell the joke to your mom and dad. They *would* have liked the joke on their own. However, this happened to be their afternoon to have tea with the local pastor and his wife.

LET'S GO, JOHN.

As your mother was washing your mouth out with soap, you might have been having second thoughts.

All that great confidence that you had built up was suddenly and completely broken down, and you never told a joke again. But this was only because you didn't know the

#1 RULE of JOKE-TELLING:

KNOW YOUR AUDIENCE!

CHAPTER 3

HOW TO REMEMBER JOKES

KNOWING YOUR AUDIENCE MAY BE THE NUMBER ONE RULE OF JOKE-TELLING, BUT WHAT GOOD IS KNOWING YOUR AUDIENCE IF YOU CAN'T REMEMBER A JOKE IN THE FIRST PLACE?

AS A MATTER OF FACT, BOB, THAT IS THE MAJOR REASON PEOPLE GIVE FOR WHY THEY DON'T TELL JOKES AT ALL. THEY SAY THAT NO MATTER HOW HARD THEY TRY, THEY JUST CAN'T REMEMBER THEM.

In this chapter I will give you twelve different techniques that will help you remember jokes. Any one of these techniques will improve your ability, but picking several that work best for you and combining them guarantees you will be able to remember any joke. You will be surprised at how well you can build up a fairly sizable repertoire in a relatively short amount of time.

At first it might require a little effort on your part, but soon these memory mechanisms will click on automatically whenever you hear a joke that you like. Remembering a joke will become second nature to you, much like riding a bike or driving a car.

Nearly every person in the world seems to know someone who is a "natural" joke-teller. When I ask people if they've heard any good jokes, they will frequently say to me, "Oh, I wish my sister was here, *she* could tell you a good one" or "You should meet this guy I work with. He comes in every day with a new joke. He's amazing! He knows a million of them."

Almost everyone knows at least one person like this:

Even though I don't write jokes, I do happen to be one of these "naturals." I have always been able to remember jokes, and I never thought that I had to make any effort to do this. I just thought that the jokes would stick in my brain by themselves.

Upon reflection, and after a number of discussions with my best joke-telling friends, I realized that natural joke-tellers do make quite an effort to retain them. There are a number of techniques that we use, but I was never previously aware that there was any method to our madness. After much careful consideration and thought, however, I was able to figure out what we do and how we do it.

By the end of this chapter, you will know the same techniques that we natural joke-tellers use. Our methods will become your methods.

I still use these techniques myself. Whether I use some of them or all of them depends on the joke—how complicated it is, and how much I want to remember it.

Which brings us to our first technique.

REMEMBERING TECHNIQUE #1:

Decide If You Want to Remember the Joke

A joke must make *you* laugh before you will want to repeat it. *You* are your first audience for any joke that you tell. It doesn't make sense for you to try passing along a joke if you didn't really like it yourself. *If You Don't Tell A Joke With Total Enthusiasm, You Will Greatly Diminish Your Chances of Getting a Laugh*.

There will occasionally be some jokes that you might laugh at but would never want to repeat, because they are sexist, racist, or just plain disgusting. Sometimes you hear a joke that is so offensive that you feel ashamed to laugh at it, but you do anyway against your better judgment

 and then hate yourself afterward.

The shock value of these types of jokes is what makes you laugh.

You are surprised that any person would have the nerve to say something that is so offensive. However, hearing a joke like this, then feeling guilty while laughing at it is a completely different situation from actually telling it yourself.

If a joke goes against your moral principles or doesn't measure up to your standards of humor, *don't tell it!*

In any event, the moment of thought that you give to a joke in order to decide whether you want to repeat it or not starts you on the road to remembering it.

REMEMBERING TECHNIQUE #2:

Ask to Hear It Again

Once a joke passes your highly selective criteria, and you decide that you actually *do* want to tell it, ask the person who told it to you to repeat it.

They will be so flattered that you liked their joke so much that you want to tell it yourself that—trust me, they will be overjoyed to tell it to you *at least* one more time . . .

Obviously, hearing a joke once and then having it immediately told back to you a second time will doubly increase your chances of remembering it.

Note: This technique works best in a one-on-one situation. If there are several people present, it may not be appropriate to ask them to all sit through the entire joke a second time around.

In this case, you can draw the joke-teller aside later, and ask them privately to tell it to you one more time. *They won't mind!*

REMEMBERING TECHNIQUE #3:

Make Mental Notes and Visualize

Immediately after someone tells you a joke, silently repeat to yourself the exact wording of phrases that they used, descriptions of characters, and any mannerisms that in your opinion made the joke funnier.

It is best to wait until the joke is over before you start doing this (unless, of course, you are hearing the joke told for the second time).

If you try making mental notes while the joke is in progress, you may find that this happens:

*For complete joke, see page 157.

Sort of defeats the purpose, doesn't it?

Don't concentrate more on remembering the joke than on actually listening to it! Otherwise you may miss important details, and then when the punchline comes, you might find yourself totally lost.

(You have to realize that asking someone to repeat a joke to you only works if you laughed at it the first time around.)

There is another way to help make the joke stay with you that can be done *while* you're hearing it. This method is visualization.

When you hear a joke, think of seeing it as a movie inside your mind and imagine as many visual details of it as you can. Then when you tell it to someone, all you have to do is roll this movie inside your head.

One easy way to help you do this is to put someone you know into a setting you are familiar with.

Whenever someone is telling you a joke, picture the characters, locations, and actions in the joke. By

doing this, you are using one of the most powerful
methods of all to stimulate your joke memory.

REMEMBERING TECHNIQUE #4:

*Repeat the Joke Back to
the Person Who Told It to You*

If someone was able to make you laugh at a joke,
they will be your best coach to help you tell it.
While listening to your delivery, they can help you
fine-tune those little nuances that are so crucial to
the proper execution of a joke.

*For complete joke, see page 152.

You may not even have to repeat the entire joke to them, but only key phrases that you want to be sure to get exactly right.

If you are, once again, in a situation where you're hearing it with several people, it is best to repeat only the parts of the joke that you think might be tricky for you to tell. In this case, you will not bother anyone else by repeating the entire joke. (Just between you and me, the other listeners might even be secretly thankful to you for helping *them* to remember the joke, too.)

REMEMBERING TECHNIQUE #5:

Rehearse

Repeat the joke to yourself, out loud if possible. Of course, if there are other people around, you might want to just go through it mentally instead of verbally.

Either way though, make sure that you practice *all* the elements that go into making that joke funny, including lengths of any appropriate pauses, physical motions that help the setup, and, especially, *rehearse the punchline*.

If you can actually speak the joke out loud, along with going over it mentally in your head, this will help you to train your body to remember it as well as your brain.

REMEMBERING TECHNIQUE #6:

Change The Joke

A musician once told me that the best way to learn how to play a musical passage on an instrument is to change it a little. This is also true of jokes. If you alter the joke somehow by switching a word, using a certain facial expression, or making it slightly different in any way from how you heard it, this will greatly help you to remember it.

*For complete joke, see page 207.

By doing this you are making the joke "your own." It is much easier to remember a joke once you have improved it because now it is no longer only a joke that someone else told to you, but a joke that has some of your own personality in it.

(There will be more on improving jokes in Chapter 5.)

*For complete joke, see page 206.

REMEMBERING TECHNIQUE #7:

Have a Test Person

Choose a friend who will be your trial audience whenever you want to tell a joke for the first time. This person ought to have a similar sense of humor as your own, but that shouldn't be too difficult to find. One of the main factors in how we choose our friends is that we like to laugh at the same things.

The other requirement for your test person is that you know them well enough to not be embarrassed if a joke bombs. That way, if the joke doesn't work you can ask them why. Together you might even be able to figure out a better way to tell it.

Talking over a joke like this with your friend is

another way to help you to remember it. Of course, if it gets a laugh in the first place (as it usually will), that alone is one of the best reinforcements of all to help you to remember a joke. Once you have successfully made someone laugh with a joke, your brain will easily and frequently bring it back to your consciousness.

If you can find a person to use for your test audience who wants to use you for the same thing, this is an ideal situation, because then you can both learn from each other. It also has the added benefit of furnishing you with someone who will always be telling you his or her newest jokes.

REMEMBERING TECHNIQUE #8:

Tell the Joke As Soon and As Often As Possible

Don't give a joke any time to slip out of your mind. When you hear a joke, try to tell it to someone else as quickly as you can.

As I pointed out in Chapter 2, the sooner you can tell a joke, the more details you will be able to remember.

Once you have successfully told a joke three or four times you will be able to remember it for days, weeks, months, and sometimes even years.

REMEMBERING TECHNIQUE #9:

Categorize the Joke

Another technique that can be helpful in remembering a joke is to put it in a category. If you hear a lawyer joke, try to think of other lawyer jokes that you know and try to imagine the best one to tell with your new one. One joke might nicely set up another, or be a good follow-up.

When you do tell two jokes together, experiment with which joke works best in the leadoff spot and which one serves as the big ending. You can even make one long joke by stringing a number of them together.

If one joke leads naturally into another one, then another then another, you will find that it becomes a very simple matter to remember a whole series of jokes.

REMEMBERING TECHNIQUE #10:

Imagine the Best Circumstances in Which to Tell the Joke

Often, when you hear a joke that you like, the first thing you think of (after you stop laughing) is "Oh, I know someone who would really get a kick out of this joke." You might think of one person or even a whole group of people.

If a thought like this does occur to you, imagine yourself in the situation where you would be telling that joke to those particular friends.

Visualizing yourself like this telling it to your friends will help you to remember the joke. Also, the next time you are with those people, you will suddenly be reminded of that joke you wanted to tell them.

REMEMBERING TECHNIQUE #11:

Think About Who Told You the Joke and Why You Liked It

Suppose you didn't use any of the previous techniques except #10. You finally see your friends after a long time and know that you wanted to tell them a joke, but just can't quite remember which one it was.

If you try to picture the person who told it to you, sometimes this will help to trigger your memory. Another way of trying to remember the joke is to think back to the feeling you had when you first heard it. What was it about that joke that made you want to share it with your friends?

Sometimes doing this will help you to recall what the joke was, or at least maybe the punchline. If you are able to recall only the punchline, you can usually work backward and reconstruct the joke.

*For complete joke, see page 190.

Your retelling, at this point, might be quite different from the original joke, but as long as the main ideas are there, you will get a laugh. Once you have been telling jokes for a little while and begin to understand why jokes work, this reconstructing process becomes fairly simple.

REMEMBERING TECHNIQUE #12:

This last technique is the most important one of all, more important than the rest of the techniques put together. Even if you use every one of the previous eleven ways to remember jokes, unless you *write the jokes down*, you will, without a doubt, forget more than you remember.

A very famous writer once told me that he could only keep five jokes in his brain at one time. If he tried to fit in more than that number, he would forget them all. It's like eating pancakes. You reach a limit where if you eat one more bite, you may lose the whole load. Whether it is five, fifty, or a hundred, we all have a limit to our joke memory.

Even *one* joke can slip through your brain cells before you know it. We've all had this experience:

As little as a few hours later, you are hanging out with some friends, and

When you try to think of it, though, all your mind can come up with is a blank.

You rack your brain, trying to remember the joke, but nothing comes. You can't even think of the

person who told it to you. You realize then, that it is probably gone forever.

Someday in the future someone else may tell it to you, but as soon as they hit the punchline you will say to them, ''Oh, yeah, I *did* hear that one. That *is* a good one.'' But by then, it's too late. They have gone to the trouble of telling you the whole joke and gotten no laugh.

The lesson to be learned from this experience is: no matter how positive you are that you will never forget this joke, no matter that you would bet your entire life savings that you will remember it, *you might not*. So

WRITE IT DOWN!

It doesn't take much time either—just a few moments to jot down several words about the joke.

You can use a small notebook that will become your joke file, or you can enter them into your computer. I have a friend who puts her new jokes under "J" in her address book. Anywhere will work, as long as it is a record that will always be easy for you to find.

If you are out somewhere and hear a good joke, a paper napkin, a matchbook, or the margin of an old newspaper will do fine for a quick note. When you get home, you can then transfer your notes to your permanent collection.

You will now have a source of jokes that you can always refer to, one that only has jokes in it that you think are funny.

How much you need to write for each joke depends on you. Some people need only the punchline, while others need the beginning of the joke or key phrases. After trying this a few times and looking at your notes and saying "Huh?" you will find that it is much better to write down a little more than you think you need, rather than what you believe to be the bare minimum.

Do not, however, write out the entire joke. If you write just enough to help you remember the setup and payoff, then you will be forced to fill in the rest with your own words. This helps not only your memory but also your delivery, giving it a much more natural feel.

I should warn you once again, that as you get better at remembering jokes, you will occasionally be tempted to not write down a "really good one" that *"of course"* you'll remember. This still happens to me. Even if the joke does stay with me for a while, as time goes by, I find myself wondering, "What was that great joke I was telling a couple weeks ago?"

Of course, there *are* some jokes that you truly will never forget, but that's no excuse for not entering them in your file. Those are the kind of jokes that you definitely want to be sure to have in your permanent collection.

BONUS TECHNIQUE

This is a bonus technique because you won't ever have to work at it. It will happen automatically. A friend once told me about some special surveillance wiretap systems. These are attached to telephones and will not record a conversation unless they are activated by certain words, such as "terrorist," "bomb," "grenade," "Wayne Newton," etc.

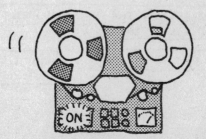

After you have been telling jokes for a while, your brain will begin to work like this. All you will need to hear is a certain word or phrase (lawyer, doctor's office, sheep) and suddenly you will find your joke center activated. You can then jump in with "That reminds me of . . . " or "Did you hear the one about . . . "

When you reach this stage of joke-telling your enjoyment will reach a new level. Jokes are much funnier and more powerful when they are put into a context. If you tell a joke that relates to a discussion you are having, or to prove a point, its humor is greatly increased.

Now that you can *remember* jokes, let's try to go out there and START TELLING them!

CHAPTER 4

BUILDING CONFIDENCE

Now it's time for you to start actually telling jokes to people. This is not nearly as difficult as it might seem at first. You just have to take small steps at the beginning to build up your confidence.

If you wanted to learn to play the piano, you would have to start slowly at first. Before you could even *think* of tickling the ivories with a hot

have to suffer through the tedious bore-

However, I am hereby very happy to inform you that delivering jokes is very different from playing the piano. You don't have to start out with simple nursery rhymes—you can tell great jokes from the very beginning. If you follow these four simple steps, you can even get big laughs from telling a joke on your very first attempt!

Step 1: Rehearse

As I mentioned before, practicing your delivery can be very helpful when you are trying to remember a joke. In order to *tell* a joke, however, especially in the beginning, rehearsal is absolutely essential! It is your only safeguard against making mistakes, and mistakes in joke-telling can be deadly.

It is very important to know the precise wording that you will use in any joke you are going to tell. Jokes are extremely delicate, and one wrong word, especially in the punchline, can quickly rob you of the laugh that you deserve. Just as you would never even think of trying to play the piano for someone without practicing first, don't tell a joke until you rehearse it.

Once again, practice the joke mentally if you like. But if at all possible, say it out loud. If you only repeat it in your mind, when you try to tell it aloud you might find that certain phrases can cause you to become unexpectedly tongue-tied.

*For complete joke, see page 186.

This can also throw off the proper timing of a joke, which is just as crucial as the right wording. All you have to do is to run through the joke out loud one or two times. Usually, this will be all you need to smooth out any trouble spots.

It really only takes a couple of minutes to practice a joke, and I guarantee you that the time and effort you put into it will be more than worth your while.

Step 2: Tell the Joke in a "Safe" Setting

This illustration shows the absolutely perfect, incomparably ideal situation in which *not* to tell a joke for the first time. The initial run through a new joke (and this goes for experienced joke-tellers as well) should be where the stakes are not very high.

Obviously, the best choice would be to tell it to someone you know quite well. If you tell the joke to a friend, you will not have to be afraid about making a mistake. If you do mess up the joke, there will be no harm done, just a brief moment of mild embarrassment.

If you are careful in choosing your first audience, though, this is where

THE FUN OF JOKE-TELLING BEGINS!!

You see, along with minimizing your risks, there is another very good reason to try out your new jokes on your friends: *It's more fun*! It can be quite pleasurable to make a stranger crack up, but it is far more enjoyable to share a good laugh with people that you know and like. Giving laughter to people you care about is one of the best reasons of all for being a joke-teller.

When you get a laugh from a joke, the laugh is your best reward. This giving of joy from one person to another is a deeply pleasurable activity, for both the person telling the joke and for the person who hears it.

When you start getting laughs from the jokes that you tell, you will need no further encouragement to continue. Everyone likes to be able to make others laugh, and *anyone* can do it! Short or tall, husky or trim, rich or poor, young or old—everyone has the ability to create hilarity around them. Telling jokes is most definitely an equal opportunity employer.

After you have gotten your first laugh from a joke, you will then know for a fact that you can make that joke funny to someone else. This will give you a greater desire and confidence to tell it again.

After telling a joke a number of times with successful results, you can even tell it to a person who doesn't laugh, without it shaking your faith in the joke or in your joke-telling ability. If you and your friends have gotten enjoyment from one particular joke, don't let another person's inability to see its humor destroy it for you. Keep telling that joke and you will see that it still has a lot more fun in store for you.

Step 3: Start with Short Jokes

One-liners are much easier to tell and are, therefore, ideally suited for the beginning joke-teller. They are less difficult to remember and are not as complicated to deliver as longer story-type jokes.

*For complete joke, see page 174.
**For complete joke, see page 151.
***For complete joke, see page 205.

This does not necessarily mean that you cannot enjoy telling a short joke as much as a long one. A one-liner can get as good a response as a long joke, and a good laugh is extremely enjoyable, regardless of how long the joke was that produced it.

Step 4: Gradually Expand to Longer Jokes

Once you have become somewhat consistent (remember, no one can ever bat 1,000) with short jokes, you can begin to try out anecdotal humor. Some people prefer to stay with one-liners all their lives—and there is nothing wrong with that—but story jokes are a lot more fun to tell.

Part of the enjoyment of jokes is in the telling of them. While you are relating a long story joke you are able to put more of your personality into it, and this makes it a much more creative experience.

THE GUY GOES FLYING UP IN THE AIR, THEN COMES DOWN ON HIS BACK!*

HE'S CHOKING, TRYING TO GET HIS BREATH AND TURNING BLUE.

FINALLY, HE MANAGES TO PULL HIMSELF UP ONTO HIS HANDS AND KNEES.

*For complete joke, see page 168.

Of course, this does make a joke somewhat riskier to tell, but when it is delivered well, the reward of laughter is much greater.

If you are interested in telling story jokes right away, then by all means try telling them. But if you do, it is advisable (even for veteran joke-tellers) to warm up your audience (and your confidence) with one or two short ones.

CHAPTER 5

IMPROVE THE JOKE

As I mentioned earlier, if you can add something of your own to a joke, it will become a part of you. Not only does this help you to remember the joke, but it also makes it much more enjoyable to tell.

Once you have started telling jokes, it won't be long before you begin understanding how humor works. When this happens, you will find that you can modify a joke to make it even funnier than it was the way you heard it originally.

This chapter will present you with seven different methods for improving jokes. Figure out which particular method (or methods) best applies to the joke you want to tell and then have fun with it!

1. ADDING A WORD OR PHRASE

In telling a joke over and over, you will usually vary it slightly from time to time. Occasionally, you will word something a little bit differently.

Now and then, you will throw in a new phrase just to punch things up a little. Sometimes this can happen by accident or might even be a mistake. However, sometimes this new embellishment will get a laugh, much to your great surprise.

The next time you tell this joke, you will, of course, add this improvement. You won't even have to try and remember it. Once you have gotten a laugh (or even a chuckle) with a new word or phrase that was your own invention, it will always, without a doubt, become one of your favorite parts of the joke. Forever after that, whenever you tell that joke, you will be chomping at the bit to use that line.

2. EXPRESSIONS AND PHYSICAL GESTURES

Expressions and physical gestures can make jokes much more enjoyable. When telling a joke try approaching it from an acting standpoint.

If you are telling a joke about someone who is confused, wear a quizzical look on your face and scratch your head.

If someone is on the phone, hold an imaginary telephone to your ear.

Be careful, though. Don't act out the entire joke. These elaborations and refinements must be handled with extreme care. *Your* style of joke-telling will usually dictate how broad your gestures should be.

For example, If you tell jokes in a low-key manner your movements should also be minimal.

On the other hand, If you are high-energy, you can flail your arms over your head if you like.

As with most of the suggestions and techniques in this book, there can always be exceptions.

If you are normally soft-spoken, sometimes wild exaggeration of movement can be used for great comedic effect.

And of course, the opposite is true.

Don't be afraid to experiment!

3. BREVITY

Another way that you will learn how humor works is that you will notice how Shakespeare was right when he said that "Brevity is the soul of wit." One thing to be aware of, as you tell jokes, is that the longer it takes to get to the punchline, the funnier that punchline has to be.

If people are going to stay with you during a long story, they are going to want a fairly hefty reward to come at the end. You can offset this great expectation by giving them little laughs along the way. If, while you are telling the joke, you can inject funny phrases, expressions, or gestures (sort of mini–punchlines), your audience will enjoy the process of hearing the joke enough so that they won't put more weight on the punch line than it can bear.

This tactic requires a fair command of the art of joke-telling, so at the beginning a general rule is to keep the story as concise and to the point as it can be. As you are telling a joke, ask yourself, "Do they need to know this to understand the punchline?"

A MAN GOES INTO A RESTAURANT. HE IS DARK-HAIRED WITH BROWN EYES AND IS WEARING A NAVY BLUE SUIT WITH BLACK WING-TIP SHOES. HE IS GIVEN A TABLE IN THE SMOKING SECTION, THEN ASKS

TO BE CHANGED TO NON-SMOKING. WHEN HE GETS COMFORTABLE, THE WAITER COMES OVER. THE WAITER IS IN HIS EARLY FORTIES, WITH THINNING SALT-AND-PEPPER HAIR. HE FILLS THE WATER GLASSES, THEN...

After a while, you will begin to understand the essential elements that make a joke work, and you will include only those points when telling it. You will also know when to leave out elaborations that will only bog down the story.

A GUY GOES INTO A RESTAURANT. WHEN THE WAITER COMES OVER TO HIS TABLE, THE MAN SAYS TO HIM...*

This too will come to you naturally the more you hear and tell jokes.

Incidentally, the ability to leave out extraneous fragments and get directly to the heart of the matter will help you with your life in general. When telling any kind of story to a friend, or explaining a situation in a business environment, you will get your point across much more effectively if you respect your listeners enough not to waste their time on superfluous details of only marginal interest. You will gain greater respect in their eyes, because you will have proven yourself to be a person of few, but well-chosen, words.

*For complete joke, see page 153.

4. HEARING VARIATIONS

When you tell someone a joke, they will usually want to return the favor, so a natural result of being a joke-teller is that you will start hearing more jokes. When this happens, you will notice that different people will try to tell you different versions of the same joke.

> A WOMAN WHO LOVES THE BEATLES GOES INTO A TATTOO PARLOR...

> A WOMAN GOES INTO A TATTOO PARLOR AND SAYS TO THE TATTOO ARTIST, "I JUST LOVE BOXING...*

Sometimes you won't even recognize that it is the same joke until just before the punchline, or it might even be during the punchline itself. When this happens, it is somewhat disappointing to you that you didn't get to hear a new joke. However, in hearing different versions of the same joke, you will often discover variations that you can use to improve the joke the next time that you tell it yourself. It might

*For complete joke, see page 202.

even be as little as a few words that help to make the joke clearer to your listener.

Sometimes, however, you hear a different way of telling a joke that can change it from a moderately funny joke into an hysterically funny one. This for all practical purposes makes it a new joke, and sometimes you can tell the joke to people a second time in its new version and get an even bigger laugh than before.

When you hear different joke variations, experiment to see which one works best for you.

5. A JOKE WORKS BETTER THAN YOU THOUGHT IT WOULD

Sometimes a joke can become more fun for you just by merely repeating it. This happens when you hear a joke that you think is funny, but only funny enough to produce a good chuckle. Then when you tell it to people they immediately respond with a hearty laugh.

Suddenly you will look at that joke in a very different light. If you keep telling the joke and it keeps getting big laughs, you will start enjoying that joke a whole lot more than you did originally. You yourself may never feel that it is a great joke, but that will not prevent you from enjoying telling it, as long as other people keep laughing.

Another way this can happen is that you might not even think a certain joke is funny enough to repeat, but you keep hearing it. It is so popular that all kinds of people keep telling it to you, and they *love* the joke.

At this point, you may have to sit yourself down and say, "OK, not everyone likes the same jokes.

"I don't think this one is that funny, but enough people do, so maybe—horror of horrors—I could be *wrong!*"

Here then is the exception to the rule of not telling a joke unless you yourself think it's funny. If enough people have shown you that they like a joke by telling it to you, you can be reasonably certain that if *you* tell it, it will get a good laugh. If it doesn't, you can always say to your non-laughing listener, "You know, I didn't think that one was so funny either."

6. ACCENTS

Another way to improve a joke is to use dialects. Different accents can make a joke much more enjoyable for both the teller and the audience. This must be done, however, with one major qualification: you must be able to imitate the accent convincingly!

Using a dialect inaccurately does not help a joke at all, and is more of a distraction for the audience than anything else. One of the reasons that a joke works is that the listener is drawn into the make-believe world that the joke creates. If the jokester is using an accent that is less than convincing, it breaks down that illusion and weakens the credibility of the joke *and* the joke-teller.

The comedian Jonathan Winters is so great at imitating accents that he went over to London and stood on a soapbox in Speaker's Corner and addressed the crowd. He was ranting and raving about politics in his best British accent. At one point, he said to the people assembled around him, "We're all Englishmen here, right?" The crowd responded with a loud affirmative cheer.

If you can do a moderately good English accent, it is all right to put it into one of your jokes when telling it to an American. However, if you try telling the joke to a British person, I recommend that you be on a par with Jonathan Winters, if you are going to include the accent. Otherwise, the Briton may be distracted and may even be offended.

Obviously, the same is true of any nationality or region. If you are in the Midwest, it is all right to imitate a "Suthin" accent, or someone from "New Yawk," but when telling a joke to someone from Tuscaloosa or Brooklyn, it would be wise to use your discretion and leave the accent out. Remember, the dignity you spare *may be your own*!

7. MAKE THE HUMOR WORK FOR YOU

As your joke-telling progresses and as you begin to learn more of the mechanics of humor in general, you will also discover how humor operates best for you *in your life*.

After a while, certain words, phrases, and inflections that you use will gradually develop into an attitude that you have while telling jokes. Before you know it and without any effort on your part, you will suddenly realize that you have originated your own joke-telling style. You won't even have to think about formulating this style because it will happen naturally.

And this is the best style for you to have: your own. It's easiest to be yourself. People can tell when you are sincere, and they can also tell when you are trying to be something that you're not.

Not only is being the person you are right now much easier, it will make your joke-telling much more natural, believable, and, therefore, funnier. Your style will develop from the inside out, smoothly and effortlessly, so just kick back, relax, and enjoy it.

Along with learning how to tell jokes to fit with your own personal way of being, you will also learn how to change jokes to make them funnier for your audience.

For example, if you tell a joke to your friends who are football fans, you tell it like this:

A GUY GOES INTO A SPORTS BAR WITH HIS DOG UNDER HIS ARM. THE BARTENDER TAKES ONE LOOK AT THE GUY AND SAYS, "HEY! GET THAT DOG OUTTA HERE!"

"WAIT A MINUTE, SIR," SAYS THE MAN, " PLEASE! MY DOG IS A REALLY BIG JETS FAN AND MY T.V. IS BUSTED. WE CAN'T WATCH THE FOOTBALL GAME AT HOME AND MY DOG WILL GO CRAZY IF HE MISSES IT..."*

*For complete joke, see page 177.

Then when you tell this joke to your friends who are into baseball, you change it to . . .

Then, when you tell it to the guys into basketball . . .

The only requirement in this joke is that the team whose name you use is not doing very well that year.

Later, in this same joke, the bartender says to the man, "If your dog goes that wild when they score a field goal, what does he do when they score a *touchdown*?" When you tell this to baseball fans, you change it to "If your dog goes that wild when the team scores a run, what does he do when they win the game?" For basketball it can be " . . . when they get the lead . . . " and then " . . . when they win?"

With a little imagination you can change this joke to fit any sport, including individual sports like tennis or golf.

This happens with many types of jokes. I heard Iranian jokes recycled as Libyan jokes, then later Khaddafi jokes became Saddam Hussein jokes. Many jokes can be adjusted to apply to whatever events are currently in the news.

Sometimes jokes about certain occupations can be changed to fit into other professional situations. A large number of jokes can be translated from one job setting to another and be equally effective.

This is because most jokes are about people, and human nature is basically the same, no matter what job a person has.

If you hear a joke about a certain occupation and can change it to fit your own job, you will get a much bigger laugh when you tell it to your coworkers.

Obviously, some jokes belong exclusively to a specific profession and deal only with concepts directly related to that world. This kind of joke is sometimes too esoteric for anyone else to appreciate.

However, if you happen to be on the *inside* of a joke like this, it is the most fun to tell. This is because you not only make the people around you laugh, but you also create a feeling of togetherness and community: *We* can enjoy this joke that nobody else could even understand!

...PUT A CHART IN FRONT OF HIM!*

*For complete joke, see page 195.

When you first start telling jokes you will most likely want to be conservative. You will find a delivery for a joke that works best for you, and you will stick with that. Once you begin to tell jokes more frequently, though, you will gain experience and confidence.

At that point you will probably want to start taking a few chances. After all, if you're going to be telling a joke eight to ten times, on the fifth rendition why not attempt to throw in a little improvement? If it doesn't work you can always go back to the old tried-and-true version. If it does work, though, the fun you had in telling it will have been greatly enriched.

Improving a joke does require sensitivity and intelligence on the part of the joke-teller. As Miguel de Cervantes, the author of *Don Quixote* said, "The most difficult character in comedy is the fool, and he must be no fool who plays that part."

Jokes are highly fragile, and great care must be taken when telling them. Because of the punchline's crucial role in the successful telling of any long or short joke, the next chapter will be devoted entirely to the most important line of every joke.

CHAPTER 6

THE PUNCHLINE

There are varying degrees of laughter, from a slight

HUH!

on one end
of the scale
to a loud

WAAAA HAAAA-
HO-HO-HO-HO-HO-
AAAAH, OOOOH!
YES! YES! YES!
AH-HA-HA-HA-HA-
HAAAAAA!

on the other.

When you tell a joke, the aim is to get as close to that second type of laughter as possible. In attempting to do this, your closest most valuable friend is

THE PUNCHLINE!

The punchline *must* be delivered correctly, or the joke will not get the laugh you are aiming for.

True, the inherent humor of a joke does have a great deal to do with how it is received by its audience. However, a punchline properly delivered allows you to squeeze as much hilarity out of a joke as it can possibly give. In order for you to be most effective when delivering the punchline, it will be helpful for you to understand why and how a punchline works.

Sydney Smith, an English writer and clergyman who lived in the late 1700s, said, "Surprise is . . . an essential ingredient of wit." What makes us laugh at the punchline is that it turns us in a different direction from where we expected to go.

When Henny Youngman says,

. . . you have already mentally filled in the phrase, "For example" into that brief momentary pause before he says, "Please." We bring a certain set of expectations to every joke that we hear, and the setup of the joke leads us "down the garden path."

Or, as Gene Perret explains it in his excellent book, *Using Humor for Effective Business Speaking*: "I liken a joke, or more specifically a punchline, to pulling a rug out from under unsuspecting victims.

You have to position them properly on the rug. That means you as the story-teller have to lead them where you want them.

You have to direct their minds in the direction you want them to go. Then you have to tug on the rug at that precise moment. If you do it too early they're not on the rug yet—you've accomplished nothing. If you let them know you're going to do it, they'll step off and again—no result. In effect, you have to outsmart your audience.''

Fortunately, when you tell a joke your audience *wants* to be outsmarted. They want to laugh. So they're hoping that you will be successful at tricking them. This desire does not, however, mean that they will totally suspend their belief in logic. If a joke doesn't make sense, the structure of the setup breaks down and the joke loses its effectiveness.

However, you wouldn't want people to allow you to be illogical because the more logical a joke is, the funnier the punchline will be. You want your audience to totally believe. They say that in judo you learn how to use the size and weight of your opponent against him. It's the same in telling jokes: create a logical world plausible enough for your listener to throw himself completely into it. Then you use the punchline to twist that logic into humor.

This does not mean that a joke cannot break the laws of nature. We have jokes about Martians, genies, people in heaven and hell, and talking animals.

No matter how way out it may seem, though, every joke has its very own sense of logic, and no matter how quirky that logic may be, you must always remain within those boundaries.

Since surprise is the main reason that we laugh at a joke, you must not in any way give the listener any clue as to what is coming. If you tip it off, even slightly, it will either ruin the joke or at best diminish the laugh you get.

This principle also works within the structure of the punchline itself. The funniest word of the punchline should always be as close to the end of the line as possible, and is almost always the very last word of the joke.

If you hear a joke that does not end with the "punch word," try to figure out a way to tell it so that it will. By shifting the wording around, you can often raise the joke several notches on the laugh meter.

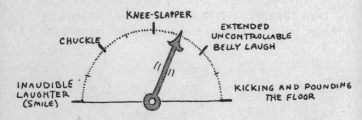

A word of caution: figuring out which word is the punch word is not always as completely obvious as it might seem. Sometimes it takes some thought and experimentation to discover where in the punchline the true humor resides.

Another extremely important element of delivering a punchline is timing. The most obvious aspect of this is that the punchline cannot be rushed. You must say it slowly and clearly enough so that your audience can understand all the words.

Beyond this, there is something called the "art of timing." This kind of timing, though, is an intangible factor in a joke that cannot be measured, not even in microseconds. It is something very difficult to teach, because the proper timing of a joke is different for every person who tells it.

To use professional comedians as examples, I would like to point out the different ways that Rodney Dangerfield and Stephen Wright deliver their material.

Rodney Dangerfield's approach is highly energetic and rapid-fire. He barrels through joke after joke without even pausing to give you time to laugh.

Stephen Wright, on the other hand, almost mumbles his jokes. He tells them so slowly that if his lines weren't so funny you would fall asleep.

Jack Benny is considered to have been one of America's greatest comedians, largely because of his impeccable sense of timing. He knew how to use silence in such a manner that he could often get uproarious laughter without saying a word! Of course, this kind of ability takes years to develop.

Since timing is so closely related to a joke-teller's personal style, it is basically a skill that must be acquired through experience. Once again, experimentation is the key. If you try out a punchline several different ways, you will quickly find the variation that works best for you.

When a person in any field (from playing the violin to laying bricks) is talked about as "having a lot of experience" what does that mean? Basically, it means that they have already made a lot of mistakes. They performed their task incorrectly enough times in enough different ways that they have learned how *not* to do it. You learn as much by doing something wrong as you do by doing it right. Sometimes you learn even more that way.

Now that you have read this far, you understand enough about the setup of a joke and how and why the punchline works. Now, the only way for you to learn how to tell jokes is to actually go out and *do* it.

The only way to expand what you know is to get out there into the world and start testing your knowledge.

Let's go!

CHAPTER 7

TELLING JOKES

Now you know many techniques to use to remember jokes, have learned how to build up your confidence, know some different ways to make jokes funnier, and are aware of the importance of a correctly delivered punchline. It is now time for me to give you some pointers on joke-telling in general, and for a discussion of several different varieties of jokes.

First of all, as you may have already noticed from hearing jokes, a good joke is almost always told in the present tense. You don't say, "A guy went into a bar and said . . . " The proper delivery is "A guy goes into a bar and says . . . " This lends a certain immediacy to a joke. It makes it feel like something that is happening right now, not something that occurred in the past.

Normally in standard grammatical usage you must be consistent. But this is not true with jokes. If you need to start a joke in the past, shift as soon as you can to the present.

MOSES CAME DOWN FROM THE MOUNTAIN AFTER TALKING TO GOD. THE PEOPLE ARE OVERJOYED TO SEE HIM SO THEY ALL GATHER AROUND TO HEAR ABOUT HIS EXPERIENCE OF TALKING WITH THE SUPREME BEING.*

This might seem a little awkward in print, but when told aloud, the shift in tense will flow seamlessly and probably go unnoticed. This is because you will be easing into the present tense, which feels far more natural for a joke.

The timing of when you tell a joke can greatly influence how big a laugh you get. If you are having a discussion, and someone says something that reminds you of a joke, this can be the ideal moment to tell it. Jokes are great fun when told on their own, but when a joke can be woven into a subject already being discussed, its humor is increased to its maximum intensity.

I have met people who claim that they do not like jokes. (Yes, these creatures do exist, but fortunately they are a rare breed.) People like this will refuse to laugh at any joke you tell them. That is, until you tell a joke that relates to what is already being talked about. Then these non-joke people will laugh harder than anyone.

This is because the joke has suddenly graduated from being just an anecdote to a story that has relevance to their lives.

*For complete joke, see page 181.

You can sometimes create this situation artificially. Charles Lamb, an English essayist and critic who was born in 1775, said: "The teller of a mirthful tale has latitude allowed him. We are content with less than absolute truth."

Making believe that the story of a joke actually happened to someone who is in the room while you are telling it is a device that has been employed for ages. (Using a person not present is considered unfair.) Even if everyone is completely aware that this is a joke, it makes it funnier for them because they can easily visualize the story if it happened to someone they know.

Your audience can also enjoy watching the subject's reaction while you are telling the story (he or she is usually squirming a little bit).

When you hit the punchline everyone will start laughing (we hope), including the person that it supposedly happened to. This person is then required by traditional law (going back thousands of years) to then say to you, "OK, very funny, ha ha. Just you wait. I'll get you back for this."

Note: Here, right away, is an exception to the present-tense rule. If you are telling the joke as though it truly happened to someone, it of course must be told in the past tense.

Other times that jokes can relate to your daily life are those occasions when you hear topical jokes. These are the jokes that have to do with current events in the news, or the ones that circulate in the aftermath of some local, national, or global tragedy.

Although you may try to resist laughing at these jokes, which are usually far beyond the bounds of good taste, every now and then one will get you.

As I mentioned earlier, sometimes you will laugh at these kinds of jokes because of their shock value. Often, though, there is a deeper reason. When a disaster occurs on a magnitude such that your city, the whole country, or the entire world hears about it, this is very difficult to deal with on a human level.

By laughing at a joke about a tragedy, the joke acts as an emotional release, enabling you to get a certain distance from it. From this standpoint, you might be able to face the problem more easily. As the French dramatist Pierre de Beaumarchais said in the 1700s, ''I hasten to laugh at everything for fear of being obliged to weep at it.'' A century later, Gustav Flaubert took it one step further. He said, ''A laughing man is stronger than a suffering man.''

Another type of joke is called a ''suck-in'' joke. Not only do these jokes seem relevant to everyday life, they try to actually pass themselves off as reality. When telling a suck-in joke it is important for you to look as sincere as possible so that the listener will not be aware that they are being set up.

A suck-in joke sucks the listener into believing that the joke is actual truth. Even if they do know it is a joke all along, there is a moment where they are sucked into giving a certain desired response.

A MAN IS IN THE MIDWEST ON BUSINESS AND HE HEARS THAT THE MEN IN THE TOWN WHERE HE IS STAYING HAVE SEX WITH PIGS BECAUSE THERE ARE NO WOMEN THERE.

AFTER A FEW WEEKS, HE GETS SO HORNY THAT HE GOES TO THE FARM WHERE THEY HAVE THE PRETTIEST PIGS. HE TELLS THE FARMER THAT HE WOULD LIKE TO SCREW ONE OF THE PIGS, SO THE FARMER GOES AND GETS A SADDLE. THE FARMER PUTS THE SADDLE ON THE PIG, THEN HE ASKS THE MAN, "HAVE YOU EVER SCREWED A PIG BEFORE?"

"NO," SAYS THE MAN.

"THEN I'LL EXPLAIN TO YOU HOW TO DO IT," SAYS THE FARMER. "NOW YOU DON'T ACTUALLY SIT IN THE SADDLE. WHAT YOU DO IS YOU GET BEHIND THE PIG AND PUT YOUR FEET IN THE...

...UH...UH... BOB, WHAT DO YOU CALL THOSE THINGS THAT HANG DOWN...?

STIRRUPS?

OH! YOU SCREW PIGS?

As you can see, Mary had to get Bob to believe that she had actually forgotten the word "stirrups" in order to lure him into saying it.

Once you have successfully fooled someone with a suck-in joke, that person will become very suspicious of you. For this reason, it will be necessary for you to wait a while before attempting to tell them another suck-in joke. You must give them time to regain their trust in you.

Then you swoop!

One other kind of joke that I would like to discuss here is the visual joke. This is the type that requires the teller to make physical gestures. Because these jokes use not only the listener's ears but also his eyes, they literally add another dimension to the humor.

An example of a simple visual joke would be:
Two eighty-year-old men are sitting on a park
bench, when one of them says to the other,

Visual jokes can be very entertaining not only for
your audience but also for you, the teller. Some of
these jokes involve elaborate movements and facial
expressions, so this allows you the enjoyment of
putting your body into your jokes, along with your
mouth. Sometimes your mouth has to put in over-
time, too, on sound effects.

Any joke that requires more from you than just
merely saying words is much more creative and is

therefore much more fun to deliver. The only drawback to visual jokes is that they can't be told over the phone!

As I said earlier, if you are going to tell several jokes in one sitting, it is best to start with a couple of one-liners or short jokes. These will serve to warm up the audience as well as yourself.

However, you should always save your best jokes for last, no matter whether they are long or short. The reason for this is that if you tell your best one at the beginning of a joke session you may set a standard that your following jokes cannot match.

When you are telling jokes in this manner (building up to the funniest one), it will occasionally happen that one of your lesser jokes will strike a person's funny bone in a way that you didn't expect and they will get hysterical with laughter. As difficult as it may be to do at this time, realize that this joke is *the* joke for that sitting, and save your other good ones for another time.

Save your other favorite jokes for the time when they will be most appreciated. I want you to know, though, that this piece of advice is definitely much easier to give than to actually follow. As a matter of fact, if you can do this you are, as they say, "a better man than I." Even though I'll know that I should stop, I will try telling a few more jokes, and get disappointing results, before I am finally able to give up.

Whenever you tell a joke to someone, it is important to make eye contact. Look directly at the person you're telling it to. Joke-telling is a form of communication, and people do not feel connected to you if you don't look them in the eye. I do not mean, however, that you have to stare them down.

But an occasional glance at their pupils will keep them with you. (Eye contact also serves to make sure that they are still paying attention.)

When telling a joke to a small group of people, look at everyone.

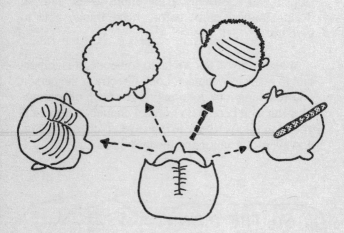

Glance briefly into the eyes of every person in the small circle, to make sure that they all feel included. When you deliver the punchline, though, look at only one person. This creates an intensity to the moment which will effectively direct the group's focus on the punchline.

When telling a joke to a very large audience, it is impossible to look at everyone, so it is best to pick several people in different locations throughout the room and spread your focus around among them. If you are on a stage with a spotlight shining in your eyes it may be impossible to see anyone beyond the first four rows (if you can even see that far).

In this case, pick a person or two up front and focus on them part of the time, and on the vast blackness in front of you the rest of the time. If you are able to see a lighted exit sign, you can pretend that it is a person and make it another point for your focus.

As long as we are talking about telling jokes to a large group, if you are ever in this situation it is wise to be conservative in your joke selection. Jokes that reach the lowest common denominator will be your best choices.

There are three reasons for this:

Reason #1 If your joke is too specifically geared to a small segment of your audience, only some people will understand it, leaving others feeling left out.

Reason #2 Let's face it, many jokes are on the borderline of good taste, while some other jokes go galloping over that line and ride for miles before stopping. Jokes on the edge of tastefulness and beyond should be avoided in front of a large audience. You don't know everyone there, so you run the risk that you might offend someone. (KNOW YOUR AUDIENCE, REMEMBER?)

Reason #3 Suppose you *did* know everyone in the audience, and knew that they would understand the joke and not be insulted by it. In all likelihood, though, everyone listening would not know everyone else, like you do. If you told an inside joke, or one that might be considered vulgar, your friends who would ordinarily laugh at the joke might be worried about other people in the audience who don't get it. This would diminish *their* pleasure, and you wouldn't be able to get the laugh that you want.

So don't take chances in front of a large crowd. Things *could* get ugly.

Finally, I want to remind you that the whole point of telling a joke is to get a laugh out of your audience.

For this reason, it is very important to let a laugh go on for as long as possible. If you are in a group of people it is especially important to be aware of this. Don't interrupt someone else's laughter by starting to tell another joke.

Stepping on another person's laugh is very rude, so wait until all the laughter has died down before you begin telling your next one. Sometimes this will take split-second timing in order to get your joke going before someone else starts theirs. It's better to make that effort, though, than to cut the fun short.

The giggles, chortles, and guffaws that we get in response to jokes are the real reason that we tell them in the first place. Sit back with everyone else and enjoy your laughs together. There's a lot more where that came from, and plenty more to go around.

CHAPTER 8

HUMOR IS SUBJECTIVE

For your own protection, it is very important for you to be aware of the fact that humor is extremely subjective. A joke that makes one person hysterical with laughter could leave another person totally cold, and might even make a third person feel offended or even angry.

This will be helpful for you to understand as you go out into the world to tell jokes. If one of your jokes does not get a laugh, it is very possible that this has nothing to do with your delivery or with the joke itself.

There are some people who are just a tough audience, and it is monumentally difficult to make them laugh. Henry Ward Beecher, a preacher and lecturer who lived in the mid-1800s, said, ''Some people are so dry that you might soak them in a joke for a month and it would not get through their skins.''

When telling jokes, it is best for you to steer clear of this type of person.

They will only frustrate you and be a waste of your energy.

Now and then you might run into people who actually think something is funny, but refuse to laugh. A certain Lord Chesterfield, an English statesman who lived in the early 1700s, is quoted as saying, ''The vulgar often laugh, but never smile, whereas well-bred people often smile, but seldom laugh. In my mind, there is nothing so illiberal and ill-bred as audible laughter.''

Believe it or not, there are still people around these days, three hundred years later, who think in much the same manner.

I know two guys who will not laugh at any of my jokes, no matter how many I tell them. Even if it looks like they might think the joke is funny, they just don't seem to want to give me the satisfaction of laughing. Now, you must understand that I tell a lot of jokes to a lot of people, and I usually get a really good response, so for the longest time I could not understand these two fellows. Since my success rate is so high with other people, I knew that the problem was not with me, even though they tried to make me think it was.

Then one day I read an interview with a famous singer, who happens to have grown up near these two guys.

This singer said that when he was a teenager it was not considered macho to laugh. He said that he and his friends would sit around and try to make each other crack up. If someone actually did laugh, it was perceived as a sign of weakness. After reading this, I finally understood where they were coming from.

Oddly enough, these two guys *do* have good senses of humor, and we kid around a lot. They always refused, though, to laugh at any of my regular jokes, until one day I surprised them. I told them a joke and put the name of their business competitor into the punchline. They both burst out laughing. When they finally settled down, one of them said, "Now, that's funny!"

This demonstrates once again how you can improve a joke by knowing your audience and changing the joke to suit them.

Sometimes it might happen that your listener is just not in the mood to hear a joke, or maybe your joke, in some unknown way, strikes too close to home for them. It might also be that they just plain don't think your joke is funny. Josh Billings, an American humorist from the 1800s, said that "There are very few good judges of humor, and they don't agree." As a joke-teller, sometimes you just have to be prepared to agree to disagree.

In an article in *TV Guide*, Jackie Gleason, "The Great One," put it this way: "Of course, one of the most horrifying aspects of comedy is the basic fact that what is funny to one person or group is not equally amusing to others. The shoe shops of the world are now full of would-be comics who never learned that. It took me some time to realize that certain things that break me up leave many of my pals stony-faced.''

Mr. Gleason could have added that if everyone had the same taste, the shoe shops of the world would also be filled with shoes of only one style.

You must be willing to understand that if a person disagrees with your taste in jokes, this does not mean that they lack a sense of humor. F. M. Colby, an American editor and essayist who lived at the turn of the century, said, ''Men will confess to treason, murder, arson, false teeth or a wig.

How many of them will own up to a lack of humor?''

Almost everyone thinks they have a good sense of humor. As a joke-teller, you should always keep this in mind.

Once you realize that everyone does have a sense of humor, the next step is to just figure out what kind they have. After you tell several jokes to an audience and see what they respond to, you will begin to see what they like. Then you can choose jokes for them that fit their particular (and/or peculiar) taste.

Keep in mind, though (to paraphrase Abe Lincoln), ''You can't make all the people laugh all the time.'' To make his original statement apply to joke-telling, you would also have to change the beginning of it to say, ''You can't make all the people laugh some of the time, or some of the people laugh all of the time.''

There is never a joke guaranteed to make everyone laugh, and there are no people who will laugh at everything. However, when you start telling jokes it will be surprising to you how often you will be able to make people laugh. If you keep telling jokes, it won't be long before you will notice that you can actually make *most* of the people laugh *most* of the time!

But now, there are a few aspects of joke-telling that I should warn you about.

CHAPTER 9

DANGERS

Now it is time for me to point out to you some of the dangers of joke-telling. Actually, "danger" might be too strong a word to use when talking about joke-telling. After all, what happens if you tell a joke and it doesn't get a laugh? Usually, the worst thing that happens is that you suffer a momentary pang of embarrassment. That's not exactly life-threatening, is it? You must realize that when you tell a joke and it falls, the only person that it really bothers is you.

No one is going to judge you on the basis of one joke that didn't go over, except perhaps in the situation where it is a first impression. One more time: KNOW YOUR AUDIENCE!

If you are telling jokes to strangers, it is always best to rely on your proven material. But if you tell a joke to a friend and it doesn't work, it probably doesn't matter. I have not heard of someone changing their opinion of a friend just because that friend told a joke that bombed.

If you tell a joke that gets little or no response, have fun with it! Johnny Carson has made an art form of converting dud jokes into big laughs.

Both Gene Perret's book, *Using Humor for Effective Business Speaking,* and Milton Berle's *Private Joke File* have a number of "savers" that can be used in this situation.

If a joke doesn't work, your audience will still be with you as long as you don't collapse onto the floor in a heap of throbbing insecurity. A joke that bombs is never a real problem, and sometimes, you can turn it into a humorous moment.

Obviously, though, you want your jokes to do well. Here are some scenarios to watch out for. Knowing about them can help you avoid hearing total silence at the end of your punchline.

For starters, the best way to kill a joke is to

OVERHYPE IT!

We have all had the experience of going to see a movie that *everybody* has been telling us for weeks is the *greatest* movie in *years*. After we have seen it ourselves, we think, "What was all the fuss about? It was good, but it wasn't *that* good."

That movie was unintentionally ruined for us by all the people who raved about it. They only wanted to have us see the movie and enjoy it for ourselves, but they inadvertently set up expectations for us that couldn't possibly be met.

I heard about the movie *Gone with the Wind* in such glowing terms for so many years that when I finally saw it, I thought to myself, "Well, it was OK, but it sure wasn't *Gone with the Wind*!"

Do not preface a joke with

Even if the joke *is* great, just say,

Let the greatness of the joke sneak up on your listener and surprise them.

Another way that you can unintentionally over-hype a joke is by giggling your way through it. By doing this you are giving the secret away, telling your listener that you think the joke is an incredibly funny one. Unfortunately, though, sometimes this situation is unavoidable.

Now and then you will hear a joke that is so funny that you just can't wait to repeat it. However, as you begin to tell it, you realize that you have not yet finished laughing at it yourself. Try as you might, you just can't keep a straight face as you say the lines. Sometimes you're working so hard to choke back the laughter that you can't even get the words out.

In this case, it just might be better to cut your losses and say,

Adding too many details, or overacting, can also build up expectations for a laugh much bigger than the joke can actually deliver.

I mentioned earlier that if you can sometimes put humorous asides into a long joke it can lessen the pressure of the punchline having to be hysterically funny. I also said that this can be a somewhat tricky procedure.

One of the reasons for this is that the laughs along the way shouldn't be bigger than the punchline. If they are, and the telling of the joke is more fun than the actual punchline, it will be a letdown for your audience.

Earlier on, I abbreviated a quote by Sydney Smith. His full statement was, "Surprise is so essential an ingredient of wit that no wit will bear repetition." Jokes are not funny the second time around. If someone tells you that they have already heard your joke, STOP! Don't force them to sit through it again.

Don't keep repeating the punchline, either.

Don't fall into that common trap of "If it's funny once, it's funnier twice." It's not, and it won't be. So move on. If your listener, however, wants to repeat the punchline, that's all right. You should

*For complete joke, see page 152.

lean back, rest on your laurels, and enjoy the laughter of your audience.

What happens when someone doesn't understand the humor of a joke?

One time I was telling a joke to a married couple that I know. When I hit the punchline, the man let out a hearty laugh. He kept laughing until his wife dropped that old killer line on us:

I then patiently explained the joke to her, at which point she said, "That's not funny."

The husband became very exasperated, obviously having been through this a number of times before. He said to her, "Of course it's not funny, dear. Once you have to explain it, it's not a joke anymore." And he was right.

If someone doesn't get your joke right away, give

him a few moments to ponder it. After all, some of
the best jokes (at least *my* favorites, anyway) are the
ones that you don't get immediately, but take a little
thought.

If you give your audience a bit of time and they
still don't get the joke, you can try prompting them
a little. If they *still* don't get it, you can go ahead and
explain it to them, but if you do, don't expect to get
a laugh.

ONCE YOU HAVE TO EXPLAIN IT, IT'S NOT A JOKE ANYMORE!

I would now like to give you another word of
caution. It is very risky to try to repeat funny lines
that you have heard from a professional comedian.
We've all had the experience of seeing something
humorous on television and then trying to tell it to
a friend the next day.

As we all know, this usually does not work. This
is because those lines were written for a specific

character or comic persona, sometimes for a specific situation in a show, and were delivered by an experienced performer. After trying to recapture all that later for our friends, most of us are left mumbling,

If you stick to generic one-liners and short jokes, you have a much greater chance of getting genuine laughs. The more ordinary jokes are ideal for people like you and me. Leave the professional comedy lines to people who pay their writers large sums of cash.

There is one other danger in the world of telling jokes that I want to warn you about. This is, unfortunately, an unavoidable experience. I bring it up only so that when it happens to you, you will know that you are not alone. This is a phenomenon called ''the pepper mill syndrome.''

The pepper mill syndrome occurs when you are at a table in a restaurant with a large group of people. You start to tell a joke, and everyone turns to listen. It starts out really well, and as you get into the joke you can see by the smiles on their faces that people are really enjoying it. You throw yourself totally into the story, using all the appropriate gestures and facial expressions, all to maximum effect. All eyes are upon you, and just as you are about to deliver the punchline, the waiter suddenly appears and says:

PEPPER, ANYONE?

It happens every time.

CHAPTER 10

FOR WOMEN ONLY

In the beginnings of modern American comedy, back in the days of vaudeville and burlesque, a strong tradition was established. Men were almost always the comedic performers in a show, and the women entertainers were usually show girls: sexy, beautiful, and dumb.

If a woman *did* perform comedy, she played a brainless, ditzy character, reinforcing an old, comfortable (for men) stereotype.

In her era, Gracie Allen was one of the most popular entertainers in the country. She perfectly fit the mold of being the spacey, almost childlike woman who needed to be taken care of. I doubt if society at that time would have let her succeed, if her bemused husband weren't constantly by her side on stage. So you can see that it was only acceptable for a woman to take control of an audience if she didn't appear to be in control of herself.

This is not meant in any way to lessen Gracie's importance to American comedy. Burns and Allen were tremendously funny, and can still be enjoyed and appreciated today, even though their comedy fit in perfectly with the standards of their era.

This is a testament to the depth and universality of their humor. Gracie herself had to be a brilliant woman to keep straight, in her own mind, the convoluted logic of her lines.

In the early 1960s the first women in stand-up comedy followed in Gracie's footsteps. The two women who were the forerunners in this field, Phyllis Diller and Joan Rivers, both had to break in by performing self-deprecating humor.

To her credit, Joan Rivers has continued to grow and evolve with the times, just as comedy itself has. By transforming her comedic persona, she succeeded in doing something extremely rare for a performer. In essence, she has had two careers: first as a helpless, ugly duckling, and second as a headstrong, confident woman. She was able to adjust her humor to fit with current styles, and she is now just as funny and relevant as she has ever been.

Phyllis Diller and Joan Rivers opened the door for women in comedy today, who are allowed to have comedic styles as varied from one another as their personalities and imaginations can make them.

Even though the world of professional comedy has opened up for women, why is it that there are still fewer women telling regular jokes in the course of their daily lives? (By this I mean the one-liners and story jokes that you hear at parties, on the job, and among friends.) Why is it that men tell jokes and women usually don't?

First of all, it is common knowledge that men, generally, are not as comfortable communicating on a deep personal level as women are. Most men don't talk as easily about their feelings.

Telling a joke is a great way to break the ice, to quickly establish contact.

Sharing a laugh is a very real form of communication, a way of feeling connected, with a minimum of risk. It does not take nearly as much social courage to say, "Have you heard the one about . . ." as it does to say, "I'd like to know you better, and I'm a little nervous."

There is a fairly logical reason why men have become like this. From as far back as the time of the caveman and the cavewoman, men have seldom been afforded the luxury of exposing their emotions in a safe environment. If a man was feeling depressed it didn't matter much to the mastedon he was about to confront with his slingshot. He still had to go out and perform—killing that mastedon for food.

It didn't matter that his child had just vomited on his favorite bearskin loincloth. He still had to fight in order to eat.

(By the way, this might be a great argument in favor of vegetarianism. How much courage does it take to pull a carrot out of the ground?

Even today, this same principle applies. Let's face it, it causes much greater stress to lay out the cash for a filet mignon dinner for two than it does to pay for a garden salad delight.)

At any rate, we can see that jokes are a great way to feel close to someone without having to risk too much in the way of therapy bills.

Even though it might generally be easier for women to connect emotionally with others, this does not mean, however, that jokes will not work as well for them or be as much fun. Not at all! Telling jokes is an enjoyable addition to any person's life and can enhance communication for everyone.

Another reason that men might take so naturally to telling jokes is that boys are trained from birth to channel their healthy aggression into sports and games. This is especially true in this country, where competition reigns supreme.

When taken to the extreme, competition can make people feel very alienated and distant from each other. You can never trust another person because he might be able to take your money from you, or your spouse, or your TV remote-control clicker.

On the other hand, it is important to remember that a healthy competitive process can give you a sense of identity, and, when successful, a feeling of real achievement. Competition can spur people

on to great accomplishments they might not be able to attain on their own.

For example, during times of peace we halfheartedly go about the struggle for the betterment of mankind. However, during war—the ultimate competition—mankind exhibits enormous energy, creativity, and togetherness unparalleled in most other human activities. (Love is another area where competition is incredibly fierce: "All's fair," etc.)

To tell a joke is, in a subtle way, competitive.

Of course, you must realize that not all men are joke-tellers either. Not even close to a majority. But when one looks at how females in our society have been conditioned, it is not at all surprising that there are very few women who tell jokes. In order to examine this further, it might be helpful, once again, to go back to the days of cavemen and cavewomen.

For biological reasons, cavewomen had to stay home to bear, deliver, and feed children, while the men would "go out with the boys," hunting for woolly mammoth.

For thousands of years this condition remained largely unchanged. Men worked to support the family outside the home, while the women remained at home. Until fairly recently, most people were quite happy with this system.

Unfortunately, an attitude developed among both sexes that because women did not do certain things, they were also unable to do these things. This continued for centuries.

Remember Lord Chesterfield? He was the English statesman who said that "proper" people never laugh out loud. Well, if you thought that was off the wall, wait till you hear what he thought of the feminine gender. On the subject of women, Lord Chesterfield is quoted as saying, "A man of sense only trifles with them, humors or flatters them, as he does with a sprightly or forward child; but he neither consults them about, nor trusts them with, serious matters."

Pretty outrageous, right? And what is worse is that you know that he couldn't have been alone in this opinion. What do you think the response would be if a man were to make that remark today? He would have to join the witness protection program before he could ever get a date again.

Fortunately, not everyone, even in Lord Chesterfield's day, agreed with him. John Wesley, who lived at the same time, criticized him and had this to say about Chesterfield: "If justice and truth take place, if he is rewarded according to his desert, his name will stink to all generations."

But change does not happen very quickly. For centuries before and after Lord Chesterfield, men and women have accepted these circumstances as "just the way things are."

But the world and our way of life is different now, and there has been a shift in how people view women and their roles in society. As usual, though, these changes are coming about because of necessity. Many women these days have entered the work force, not out of desire but out of a need for survival.

Women are now working as, among other things, welders, soldiers, executives, and firefighters, all previously the exclusive domain of men. So why can't women be joke-tellers, too?

Admittedly, things have not progressed to this degree everywhere in the world, or even in this country. Things are changing in the usual manner for our species: very slowly.

Even if you are the most modern, sophisticated, liberated woman, you have still been somewhat affected by these outdated attitudes. As recently as 1963, Arlene Dahl wrote a book titled *Just Ask a Man*. In it (and remember, this is *not* satire) Ms. Dahl says, "The successful female never lets her competence compete with her femininity. Never upstage a man. Don't top his jokes, even if you have to bite your tongue to keep from doing it."

As you can see, even if a woman didn't get this kind of training herself, her mother might have. In many cases, these attitudes have, to some degree, filtered down to the daughter.

Harriet Goldhob Lerner, in an article which originally appeared in the *Women's Review of Books*, said about Ms. Dahl's book, "It was written before the second wave of feminism, at a time when girls and women were encouraged to offer men narcissistic protection by feigning weakness, dependency, and incompetence when we were not fortunate enough to possess these traits naturally.''

The prevailing attitude still sometimes seems to be that if a woman is too clever or cunning, men might see her as threatening. In order to understand why men might react in this manner, let us return once more to our cave couple.

Men are physically larger and therefore usually stronger than women. This is the reason that the men went out to hunt, along with the fact that they were (and still are) ill-equipped for pregnancy and breast-feeding.

If one of these early women did not have a man to take care of her, she could likely find herself in big trouble. Women thus had to make themselves attractive to men in any way that they could, in order to survive.

If a woman in those days *was* strong, a man might be afraid of her, not because she could possibly club him on the head, but for an even scarier reason. If she could bear and raise the children, *and* get her own food, what would she need *him* for? This would leave the man feeling almost as useless as an American vice-president.

To this day, the emphasis for most women seems to be on relationships, whereas men seem to be very concerned with achievements. You can even see it in the way children play. Girls play "relationships" (dolls, house, etc.) and boys play "war" games (cowboys, football, etc.).

However, the reality of our roles is changing. A woman in today's world does not have to be physically large and strong in order to support herself. Single mothers are proving that they can raise children on their own, even though it does require the daily energy output equivalent of a small power plant.

Since men see things more in terms of accomplishments rather than feelings, it might be hard for them to immediately see that women do need them. Sometimes men aren't fully conscious of the fact that any person (man or woman) needs a creative outlet and emotional fulfillment in order to be truly happy. However, men do know this on some level, otherwise they wouldn't feel so threatened about losing a woman's love.

Telling jokes is a wonderful opportunity for women and men to share laughs with each other and to communicate on the same level.

Of course, there will still be some men who will be uncomfortable with this, because it breaks a woman out of her traditional role. In order for a woman to tell a joke, she cannot be quiet and demure. This is not a receptive, intuitive activity. In order for a person to tell a joke, she (or he, for that matter) must command attention and take control.

But now that women are beginning to be accepted more as equals in the world, they can start to allow their natural aggressive impulses to flow more creatively. When viewed from this perspective, joke-telling seems ideally suited for women. According to the laws of nature, a female must be able to give a child warmth and nurturing in order to preserve the species. What better way is there to make someone feel alive, feel truly human, than to make them laugh?

Joseph Addison, an English essayist who lived in the late 1600s, said, ''If we may believe our logicians, man is distinguished from all other creatures by the faculty of laughter.''

In the novel *Stranger in a Strange Land* by Robert A. Heinlein, the alien from outer space feels that he has finally begun to understand earth people when he begins to laugh.

Laughter makes life worth living, and women, as mothers, are the givers of life. For this reason, it should be a very natural activity for them to tell jokes. One of the greatest strengths that women have always had is their enormous capacity for making people feel cared for and secure. Josh Billings said, ''Laughter is the sensation of feeling good all over and showing it in principally one spot.'' By telling jokes, women can create laughter whenever and wherever they choose, providing us all with one of our most basic human needs.

CHAPTER 11

CREATE A JOKE NETWORK

JIM, NOW THAT WE'RE READY TO TELL JOKES, JANE AND I HAVE ONE MORE QUESTION.

THAT'S TRUE! WHAT WE NEED TO KNOW IS <u>WHERE</u> WILL WE FIND ALL THE JOKES THAT WE'RE GOING TO TELL?

THAT'S A VERY GOOD QUESTION AND I'M GLAD THAT YOU ASKED.

Obviously, joke books are a good source, and of course I can highly recommend *The New York City Cab Driver's Joke Book*. However, the best and most enjoyable way to find new jokes is to create your own network of joke-tellers.

Once you have started telling one-liners and story jokes, you will be drawn to others of the same ilk; and they will be drawn to you. The number of these people in your life will grow until eventually you will have several friends (at *least*) with whom you exchange jokes on a regular basis.

Your best tool for this activity is the telephone. As soon as you hear a good joke, pick up your phone and try to be the "first on your block" to tell the new one going around.

People might start calling you, too, but even if they don't you should call them when you have a new joke. I have several friends who never call me with jokes. They don't think about it, and that's just the way some people are. I don't mind, though, because when I call them, they are delighted to hear my new jokes and they always respond with the most recent ones they have heard.

When you're spreading these jokes around, don't

ever worry about a joke being old. There is a very true saying that goes "There is no such thing as an old joke if you've never heard it." Occasionally, you will be telling a "new" joke that you really like and discover that it was making the rounds twenty or thirty years ago! Jokes often go in cycles, and if you didn't catch a joke the last time it came through town, hopefully you'll get it this time around, or maybe the next! As long as you keep telling them, the good ones will eventually reach you.

When you begin building up your joke network, you may find that one of your joke connections is one of those people who has "heard them all." Every time that you start to tell them a joke, you only get one or two sentences into it before they jump in with the punchline. Having this happen frequently with the same person can get to be pretty frustrating for you. But because people like this know so many jokes, they are your best sources. And when you do tell them one that they haven't already heard, it will make your week!

If you happen to work in an office, you are in an ideal setting for exchanging jokes.

You can probably find at least one other joke-teller among your coworkers. If you start exchanging jokes with that person, the two of you will begin to look forward to coming in to work with new jokes for each other. This will improve the atmosphere in your office for everyone.

Sometimes you will be surprised at how you can find fellow joke-tellers in the most unusual places. Some people tell jokes that you would never expect, and often can be people with whom you have no other basis for communication.

The value of having a sense of humor in common with another person, however, should never be underestimated. Gelett Burgess, an American humorist and illustrator, said, ''To appreciate nonsense requires a serious interest in life.'' A person needs intelligence to grasp the subtle complexities of humor, and when you find a soul mate in the humor department, this is a real treasure.

For some unexplained reason, some weeks will be extremely dry, with no new jokes at all. During other weeks you will hear so many that you can't keep track of them. Sometimes this can be related to what is happening in the news.

I have one friend who always says the same thing when I start to tell him a joke that has to do with a current event. I will call him up and say, ''What do you call a person who comes from (name of a location where a recent catastrophe has occurred)?'' My friend responds every time with

He knows that this is the beginning of an onslaught of jokes on that subject. Sometimes I will call my sister in Florida with a brand-new joke relating to a newsworthy item. She will be amazed, saying, ''I can't believe it! That just happened today! Wow! New York is really incredible!''

New York is pretty amazing, but that brings us to the next question: Where do jokes come from in the first place?

How and where jokes originate is a topic of much curiosity and speculation. I have managed to trace the origins of many of the current-event type of jokes back to Wall Street. Many people had told me this, and then one day I finally met one of the traders who informed me that when business is slow, he and his friend stand around and try to make up jokes.

He also told me that for traders, jokes are good for business. If a stockbroker is on the telephone with someone and expects some action to start soon, he will begin telling jokes to the other person, just to keep him on the line.

When the trading starts, the broker is already talking on the telephone with the person he needs to contact, before anyone else.

When the stock market crashed in 1989, I thought

that it would be interesting to see how many jokes would come out of that situation. This was a tragedy that seemed tailor-made for traders' jokes. It was the exact kind of disaster that they would normally make jokes about, and more than that, this was a subject they knew intimately. I also thought that it would be interesting to see how well they could laugh at themselves.

The answer was: not very well at all. I only heard three jokes about the crash, and only one was any good.

Q: What's the difference between a stockbroker and a pigeon?

A: A pigeon can still make a deposit on a brand-new BMW.

As far as regular story jokes are concerned, where they come from is a complete mystery to me. No one seems to know. I have a friend who writes for a famous comedy star who says that even they don't have a good theory about the origin of the most everyday sort of jokes.

A few people have told me they've heard that jokes are made up in prisons. That seems to make some sense. Sitting around with nothing to do and lots of time on your hands (no pun intended) seems like a situation that lends itself to thinking up funny stories. However, if I were in prison, I don't think that I would be in the frame of mind to create amusing anecdotes, so I remain unconvinced.

If anyone actually knows a brilliant joke originator, please write to me in care of Avon Books and tell me about them. Maybe we can clear up this longstanding mystery.

There is one other very enjoyable way to collect jokes that I would like to tell you about, and that is the joke party. I got most of the jokes in my first book from the passengers in my taxicab. Just before I was ready to actually write the book, though, I decided that I wanted to round out my collection.

What I did was this: I invited all my best joke-telling friends over to my home with one purpose in mind, and that was for us to all sit around in a circle and tell jokes. After everyone had arrived, I started it all off by telling a joke that I had recently heard.

Like horses out of the starting gate, this set everyone off, with the jokes pouring out in a steady, free-flowing stream, with just barely enough pause between jokes for laughter. The atmosphere was truly charged. Everyone sat on the edge of their seats, eager to tell the next joke. The rhythm built into a contagious hysteria.

The party lasted for hours, and when it was over, all the participants left exhilarated. It was so enjoyable for everyone that I have one of these ''joke-a-thons'' every six months or so, just for the fun of it.

The rule for my parties is that only joke-tellers are allowed to attend. I don't want some non–joke-telling person to start getting bored.

Joke-tellers, when gathered together with those of their own kind, can continue indefinitely. (Occasionally, I will make an exception and let a non–joke-teller come to the party if he or she has a particularly good laugh).

These parties have grown in size and reputation, and each party has become progressively larger. At the last Joke-a-thon I had over twenty hard-core joke-tellers.

If you want to have a joke party, you don't have to be as strict as I am with your attendance requirements. You can invite as many non–joke-tellers as

you like, as long as you have three or four good
solid jokesters among you. Sit yourselves in a circle
and let those joke-tellers get started. Everything else
will take care of itself. One joke will lead to the
next, and after a while, they will be unstoppable.

When I have my parties, I add a couple of little
extra touches that you might or might not want to
include.

At the beginning of each party, I announce that I
have written down the punch line of a specific joke
on a piece of paper. If, in the course of the evening,
someone tells that joke, he or she will win a prize.
(A rubber chicken or a pair of nose glasses I think
are quite appropriate.)

I also hand out pencils and small pads of paper to
everyone. This is because I have noticed that something always happens when jokes are being ex-
changed. If a person is telling me a joke, while I'm
listening to it I will usually be reminded of a joke
that I want to tell him. However, by the time he

reaches the punch line of his joke, I have already forgotten mine.

By handing out the notepads, if someone thinks of a joke they are able to make a note for themselves and not forget it. By doing this, I maximize the potential number of jokes told at the party. An added benefit of the pads and pencils is that people can also use them to make notes to help remember all the great jokes they hear at the party.

You don't really need to provide pads and pencils in order to have a successful joke party, or give a prize for telling the mystery joke. It wasn't until the third or fourth party that someone finally won the rubber chicken (even though I always picked the punch line from the joke I had heard told most often in the weeks preceding the party). No one seemed to mind that it took so long to win. The real prize has always been the opportunity to share so much laughter with fun and funny people.

Before one of my parties, I bought a couple of six-packs of beer to offer my guests. As soon as my friends walked in the door, though, the joke-telling began and I completely forgot about the beer. Several hours later, after the last people had left the party, I went to the refrigerator to get something to drink. When I opened the door I saw all the beer cans still sitting there. I got really angry at myself for not being a good enough host to even think about offering it to anyone.

Then suddenly it dawned on me. I just had a party for three or four hours where everyone was laughing and totally involved and there was no alcohol and no drugs.

There was, however, frequent hysterical laughter throughout the entire evening, and it was perfectly obvious that everyone had had a great time. It was at that moment that I fully realized how truly powerful joke-telling can be.

There isn't a person on earth who doesn't like to laugh, and comedy is extremely popular everywhere. We can find humor in movies, television, theatre, music, and nightclubs. In the last several years there has been an enormous increase in the popularity of comedy. Comedians have now entered the ranks of our cultural heroes, along with movie stars, musicians, artists, sports figures, and powerful world leaders. Maybe one of the reasons for this is that our civilization has become so stressful and so complex that the release that laughter gives to people has evolved from a luxury to a necessity.

By giving us laughter, the joke-teller is providing us with something we find extremely valuable. People spend money on comedy even at times when funds are extremely tight—*especially* at those times.

Telling jokes is a marvelous way to bring more humor and laughter into your daily life. Rather than just sitting back and passively getting fed by some star performer, jokes allow *you* to be the comedian, and bring you in contact with real live human beings! Jokes give you the opportunity to be creative, connect with others, and to give people much-needed moments of joy and happiness.

One of the most wondrous characteristics of laughter is that by giving its gift, you get something back: real, tangible proof that you are accepted. You cannot successfully make someone laugh without it also having the side effect of making you feel good about yourself.

Jokes have greatly improved my life, and they can improve yours. All you have to do is go out and tell them!

WHICH REMINDS ME, DID YOU HEAR THE ONE ABOUT...?

JOKES

A man and woman are getting undressed on their wedding night, when the bride says to the groom, "Be gentle with me, honey. I'm a virgin."

The husband is totally shocked. "How could you be a virgin?" he asks. "You've been married three times already!"

"I know," replies the wife, "but my first husband was an artist, and all he wanted to do was *look* at my body. My second husband was a psychiatrist, and all he wanted to do was *talk* about it. And my third husband was a lawyer, and he just kept saying, 'I'll get back to you next week!' "

●

Last night I slept like an attorney. First I lied on one side, then I lied on the other.

●

A surgeon, an architect, and an economist are having a discussion, and they are arguing about whose profession is the oldest.

The surgeon condescendingly says to the other two men, "Well, you know that God took a rib out of Adam to make Eve, so I think that it is rather obvious that surgery is the oldest profession."

"Ah," says the architect, "but before that, out of total chaos, God made the heavens and the earth. So I thinks it's quite obvious that architecture is the oldest profession."

The economist merely folds his arms and smiles serenely. "And where," he asks, "do you think the total chaos came from?"

●

Q: What time is it when you go to the dentist?

A: 2:30.

●

Miss Smith, a society matron in Mobile, Alabama, has a problem. Several of her young female charges do not have dates for the big debutante ball coming up. Miss Smith tells the girls not to worry, that she will think of something to do about this.

She finally decides to call the nearby military base. When she is put through to the commanding officer, she says, "Sir, my name is Miss Smith and I am having a debutante ball this Friday night. Unfortunately, a few of my girls don't have dates for the dance, and I was wondering: would you be able to send a few of your officers over on Friday evening at eight o'clock?"

The commanding officer says to the woman, "Why, yes, I think some of our officers would love to attend your little soiree."

"Thank you so much," replies the woman. "And by the way, I do have two conditions."

"Yes?" asks the officer.

"Well," says Miss Smith, in her finest Southern-belle accent, "first, I want the men to be dressed in their finest dress whites, looking just as sharp as can be. My second condition is, of course, no Jews."

"It will be arranged," says the commander.

Friday night arrives and the girls are all in the ballroom of the country mansion, dressed in their formal gowns. Several of the girls are without dates, standing alone.

Suddenly, a jeep pulls up in front of the building. Six large black officers get out of the jeep, dressed in their finest white formal uniforms.

Miss Smith hurries over to them and says, "Can I help you men?"

One of the officers says, "Why, yes, ma'am. We're here for the dance."

"Why ... why ... " stammers Miss Smith, "there must be some mistake!"

"Ma'am," says one of the officers, "*you* may make mistakes, and *I* may make mistakes, but Colonel Goldberg, *he* doesn't make mistakes."

•

Q: Why don't the Chinese use telephone books?

A: *Because with all those Wings and Wongs, they're afraid that they might wing the wong number.*

•

A really shy man and a really shy woman get married. On their wedding night, they are so modest that they get undressed separately, with each of them hidden safely from the other's view by dressing partitions. As he starts to disrobe, the groom nervously says to his wife, "Now, don't you look,"

"I won't, honey," replies the bride as she begins to unzip her dress from behind her partition. "Don't you look, either!"

The husband assures his wife, "I won't, sweetheart."

The woman gets out of her clothes, and then she picks up the bright red negligee that she had bought especially for this occasion. She had sent it out to the cleaners, and now that she picks it up, she sees that it has come back all rumpled and faded.

The bride cries out with great disappointment, "Oh it's all *pink* and *wrinkly*!"

The shocked groom yells out, "I *told* you not to look!"

•

Q: What did the Zen master say to the hot-dog vendor?

A: *"Make me one with everything."*

•

A young man is trying to hitchhike in Washington, D.C. He is very surprised to find that every time a car pulls over, the driver inside asks him, "Are you a Republican or a Democrat?"

The hitchhiker always replies truthfully. He says, "I'm a Democrat." Upon hearing his response, the drivers immediately hit the gas squealing their tires, and leave him in a cloud of dust. This happens four or five times and finally the man begins to get the picture.

The next car that pulls over is a hot-looking convertible with a beautiful blonde woman in the driver's seat. The woman looks at the hitchhiker and asks lasciviously, "Are you a Republican or a Democrat?"

The young man replies eagerly, "I'm a Republican!"

"Get in!" says the woman.

As they begin driving, the man can't keep his eyes off the beautiful blonde. Her long hair is waving in the breeze, and the wind is blowing her blouse open, partially revealing her breasts.

Suddenly the man cries out, "STOP THE CAR! STOP THE CAR!"

The woman slams on the brakes and skids off the side of the road to a sudden stop. "What happened?" She exclaims. "What's the matter?"

The young man, perspiring profusely, replies, "I've only been a Republican for five minutes, and *already* I feel like screwing somebody!"

●

Did you hear about the Polish godfather? He made someone an offer they couldn't understand.

●

A man in a restaurant calls his waiter over. "Waiter," says the man impatiently, "it's much too hot in here. Turn on the air conditioner!"

"Right away, sir!" says the waiter, and hurries to the back room.

A little later the customer calls the waiter over

again, and angrily says to him, "Waiter, now it's too cold in here. Turn the air conditioner off!"

Once again, the waiter replies, "Right away, sir!" and hurries to the back room.

In just a short while, the man calls the waiter over a third time, and at this point he is furious. "Waiter, now it's too hot in here again. TURN THE AIR CONDITIONER BACK ON!"

"Right away, sir," says the waiter, once more.

As he is hurrying toward the back room, another customer calls him over and says quietly, "Say, isn't that man over there driving you crazy?"

"No," replies the waiter in a low voice, "I'm driving *him* crazy. There *is* no air conditioner."

●

Q: What's the difference between karate and judo?

A: Karate is a martial art, and judo is what you use to make bagels.

●

A man having trouble with his sink calls the plumber to his house. After the plumber looks at the pipes, he leans back and tells the man, "I can fix the problem, but before I start, I want you to know that my fee is $150 per half hour."

"$150 a *half* hour!" says the startled man. "Why, I'm a brain surgeon, and I only get $150 for a full hour."

"Hey, don't feel bad," says the plumber sympathetically. "When I was a brain surgeon, I didn't get any more than $150 an hour, either."

●

Q: How do you titillate an ocelot?

A: Oscillate its tits a lot.

A man is sitting alone at a bar one night when a woman comes in and sits down at the bar a few stools away. When he looks at her, she starts batting her eyes at him. The next time he looks over she gives him a big smile and motions for him to come sit next to her.

The man gets up and moves over to the stool next to hers. When he sits down, the woman says "Hi, there, cutie."

"Uh, hi there," is the man's response.

"I'm a working girl, if you know what I mean and I think you're pretty cute," says the woman as she slowly winks at the man. "Tonight is pretty slow, so I'm going to give you a special one-time offer." She puckers her lips and throws him a little kiss. "For fifty dollars, I will do anything that you want, as long as you can name it in three words."

"Anything?" asks the man incredulously.

The woman leans in close to the man, looks deeply into his eyes and whispers, "Anything."

The man takes out his handkerchief, wipes his brow, and says, "Wow!"

The woman, in a low, sultry voice, repeats, "Just name it in three words."

The man sinks deep into thought. Suddenly, he brightens, "I've got it," he says. "Three words, right?"

"Three words," replies the woman as she moves in so close that their bodies are touching.

"O.K.," says the man. "Here goes: PAINT . . . MY . . . HOUSE."

Three guys are talking about bars in their respective hometowns. The first guy, an Irish man says proudly, "Up in Boston, we've got this place called Paddy's. If you go into Paddy's and buy your first drink, then buy a second drink, Paddy will give you the third one on the house!"

The next guy, an Italian from New York, says "Well, in Brooklyn we've got this place called Vinnie's. Now if you go into Vinnie's and buy two or three drinks, Vinnie will let you drink the rest of the night for free!"

The third guy, a Polish man, says, "Well in Chicago, we've got this place called Bob's. When you go into Bob's, you get your first drink for free, your second drink free, your third drink free, and then a bunch of guys take you into the backroom and get you *laid*. All for free!"

"Wow!" says the Irish guy. "That's really re-markable."

"Yeah!" says the guy from New York. "That's incredible! Did that actually happen to you?"

"Well," replies the Polish guy, "it didn't happen to me personally but it happened to my sister."

●

Q: Why does it take four women with PMS to change a light bulb?

A: IT JUST DOES!

●

Three young boys are talking about what they did on their last vacation, when one of the boys says, "You know what? I got baptized!"

One of the other boys says to the first one, "Wow, that's amazing. I got baptized, too! What religion are you?"

The first boy says, "Well, I went to the church and they sprinkled me with holy water, so now I'm Catholic! What religion are you?"

The second boy explains, "They took me down to the river, dunked me in it, and now I'm a Baptist!"

The two boys turn to the third kid and ask him, "Have *you* ever been baptized?"

"No," he says with disappointment, "I haven't."

The other two immediately say to him, "Oh, you *have* to do it, it's great." Suddenly the first boy has an idea. "Wait a minute!" he says. "*We'll* baptize you."

Upon hearing this, the third kid brightens up. "Great!" he says.

So they take him into the bathroom and dunk his head down into the commode. When he comes up, his head is dripping wet, and he says, "That was fantastic! But now, what *am* I? They sprinkled one of you with holy water and you were a Catholic, and they dunked the other one in the river and you became a Baptist. But now, what am *I*?"

"Oh, yeah," say the other two, "what *are* you?" They think about it for a minute or two, when all of a sudden the first boy says excitedly, "*I* know! You're Episcopalian!"

●

Q: Did you hear about the bulimic bachelor party?

A: *The cake comes out of the girl.*

●

A man is walking down the street when a bum comes up to him and asks for a dollar. Being in a generous mood, the man pulls out a ten-dollar bill. As he hands it to the bum, he says, "You're not going to use this for booze, are you?"

"I never drink," replies the bum solemnly.

"I hope you're not going to use it for gambling," says the man.

"I never gamble," the bum says in earnest.

"Say," says the man, "would you mind coming home with me? I would really like for my wife to meet you."

"Me?" says the surprised bum. "Why me?"

"Well," The man explains, "I would just like for my wife to see what happens to a man who never drinks or gambles."

●

An out-of-towner driving east on 46th Street at Madison Avenue pulls his car up next to a New Yorker and asks, "How far is it to Fifth Avenue?" The New Yorker considers it for a moment, then tells him, "The way you're going, about 24,000 miles."

●

A cab driver says to a beautiful woman in his taxi, "If I gave you some money, would you sleep with me?"

The woman angrily replies, "How *dare* you?"

But before she can say any more, the cabbie quickly says, "Wait a minute, lady, wait a minute! Before you get all upset, let me ask you one question. If I was as handsome as a movie star, had the body of a champion athlete, was one of the wealthiest men in the world, and I offered you two million dollars to spend one night with me, *then* would you sleep with me?"

The woman sits back and thinks for a minute. "Well," she says, "if you were *all* that then I guess that I have to admit that I would."

"In that case," says the driver, "will you fuck me for twenty-five bucks?"

"What?" says the woman. "Just what kind of woman do you think I am?"

"We've already established that," replies the cabbie. "Now we're just dickering over price."

●

Q: What's a 10 in New York City?

A: A 2 with a good apartment.

●

Two middle-aged Jewish men are talking. One says to the other, "You know, last weekend I had a *good* Shabbus."

"I'm glad to hear it," says his friend. "It's always nice when you can have a good day on the Holy Sabbath. What did you do?"

"Well," says the first man, "On Friday night all the children came home and spent the night. Saturday morning we all got up, put on our finest clothes, and went to temple. It was a very beautiful, moving service.

"Then we went back to the house, had bagels and lox, and shared family stories. Then I rented the movie, "The Ten Commandments" and we all sat down as a family and watched it together. It was a *good* Shabbus."

"As a matter of fact," says the other man, "Last weekend I had a good Shabbus, too."

"You don't say?" replies the first man. "What did you do?"

"First of all," says the other man, "a friend of mine and I went to a bar and got rip-roaring drunk. Then we went to a brothel and got ourselves a couple of hookers. Then we took them to a cheap, sleazy hotel. I screwed one, and my friend screwed the other. Then we did a switch. I did his and he did mine. Then I went home and screwed my wife until I fell asleep. It was a *good* Shabbus."

"How can you call that a *good* Shabbus?" says the first man, staring at his friend in shocked disbelief. "That's a *great* Shabbus!"

•

Q: What do you call a sleep-walking nun?

A: *A roamin' Catholic.*

•

Q: Why don't cannibals eat clowns?

A: *They taste funny.*

•

A man walking down the street sees a restaurant with a sign over it. The sign reads:

WE PAY *YOU* $500 IF WE CAN'T FILL YOUR ORDER.

So the man goes into the restaurant and sits down. He calls the waitress over and says, "Miss, I would like to order an *elephant ear sandwich*."

The waitress replies, "Just a moment, sir," and rushes back to the kitchen. She goes straight to the manager and informs him, "Well, you had better get ready to pay that five hundred dollars."

"Why?" says the surprised manager. "What's wrong?"

The waitress then tells him, "Some guy just walked in and ordered an elephant ear sandwich."

"OH, NO," cries the manager, clutching his head. "Did we run out of elephant ears?"

"No," says the waitress. "But we ran out of those big buns we serve them on."

●

Two lawyers are standing at a bar having a drink together. Suddenly a beautiful woman walks into the room. One of the lawyers leans over to the other one and whispers, "Man, I sure would love to screw *her*."

The other lawyer whispers back, "Out of what?"

●

Q: What's black and brown and looks good on a lawyer?

A: A Doberman.

●

One day, a second-grade teacher says to her class, "Children, can any of you tell me where Jesus was born? How about *you*, Billy?"

Billy begins to think. "Ummm ... ummm ... was it Pittsburgh?" he asks.

"No, it wasn't Pittsburgh," says the teacher.

"Philadelphia?" asks Billy.

"Not Philadelphia, either," replies the teacher. "It was in Bethlehem."

"Darn!" says Billy. "I *knew* it was in Pennsylvania."

●

Q: What's the difference between a Rolls-Royce and an airline stewardess?

A: Not everyone has been in a Rolls-Royce.

●

A man dies and goes to heaven. As Saint Peter is welcoming him at the pearly gates, the man confesses, "To be quite honest, Saint Peter," he says, "I'm really surprised to be here."

"Why is that?" asks Saint Peter.

"Well, to tell the truth," says the man, "I never believed in this place. I never thought that it really existed."

"That doesn't matter, my friend," replies the saint. "You see, you were a good man, you were very generous, and you helped a lot of people. Up here, that is all that matters. It doesn't matter what you believed, as long as you led a decent, moral life."

Saint Peter continues, "I do have *one* problem, though. I'm just not quite sure where to put you."

"What do you mean?" asks the man.

"Do you see that big golden mosque over there?" says Saint Peter, pointing to a cloud bank on his right. "That's for the Moslems. That big marble temple in the cloud bank behind you is for the Jews, and that big wood-carved church over there is for the Presbyterians."

Saint Peter begins pointing all around. "The Hindus are over there, Episcopalians over there ... "

"Saint Peter," the man interrupts, "what's that big, tall, black building in that cloud bank behind you?"

"Oh," says Saint Peter, "that's for the Catholics."

"But why doesn't it have any doors or windows?" asks the man.

"Well," says Saint Peter, lowering his voice, "that's because *they* think they're the only ones up here."

●

Q: What's the definition of mixed emotions?

A: Seeing your mother-in-law driving off a cliff in your brand-new Porsche.

●

A woman is sitting in a bar, buying drink after drink, and crying. The bartender goes over and tries to console her.

"What's the matter, miss?" he asks.

Through her tears she replies, "Last week my husband died and today I found out that he left me with three million dollars."

The bartender tries to comfort her, "I can understand that you're upset, but look at the bright side. You're young and now you have all this money."

"I know," cries the woman, "but my husband was so wonderful. I'd give *ten thousand dollars* if I could have him back."

●

Q: Did you hear what charge they finally got Old King Midas on?

A: *Gild by association.*

●

A seven-year-old boy is sitting at the dinner table with his parents. Suddenly he announces, "Me and Janie are going to get married!"

"Oh?" says the mother. "And how old is Janie?"

"Five," replies the boy.

"Well," says the father, "what are you going to do for money?"

"I get fifteen cents a week allowance," says the son, "and Janie gets ten. We figured that if we put them together, we'd be OK."

"I see," says the father. "But what are you going to do if you have children?"

"Well," says the boy, "so far, we've been lucky."

●

A young Jewish man falls in love with a Native American woman and they decide to get married. When his mother hears the news, however, she is extremely distressed because, of course, she wanted him to marry a nice Jewish girl.

When she hears that not only is he marrying this girl, but has decided to live with her on a reservation, the mother becomes so upset that she refuses to even speak to the boy, practically disowning him.

After a year, the son telephones the mother to tell her that he and his wife are expecting a child. The mother is happy for him, but there is still quite a bit of tension in the air.

Nine months later, the son calls the mother again. "Mom," he says, "I just wanted you to know that last night my wife gave birth to a healthy baby boy. I also want you to know that we talked it over and have decided to give the boy a Jewish name."

Upon hearing this, the mother is overjoyed. "Oh son, this is wonderful," she gushes. "I have been waiting for this moment all my life. You have made me the happiest woman in the world."

"That's great, mom," replies the son.

"And what," asks the mother, "is the baby's name?"

The son proudly replies, "Smoked Whitefish!"

Q: Where can you get a good cheddar in Israel?

A: Cheeses of Nazareth.

●

Two executives working in the garment center are having lunch together. Goldstein says to his friend, "Last week was one of the worst weeks of my entire life."

"What happened?" asks Birnbaum.

Goldstein moans, "My wife and I went to Florida on vacation. It rained for seven days and seven nights, so my wife went out and spent thousands of dollars on the credit card. I came back to New York and found out that my rat brother-in-law accountant has been ripping me off for millions. And to top it all off, when I came in to work on Monday morning, I found my son shtupping my best model on my desk!"

"You think you had a bad week?" responds Birnbaum. "My week was even worse! I went to Florida on vacation with my wife and it rained for seven days and nights, so my wife went out and spent thousands on the credit card. Then when I got back to New York I found out that my rat cousin accountant has been ripping me off for millions. To top it all off, when I came in to my office on Monday, I found my son shtupping my best model on my desk!"

"How can you say that your week was worse than mine?" asks Goldstein. "It was identical!"

"Shmuck!" replies Birnbaum. "I manufacture men's wear!"

●

Q: Did you hear about the Polish jazz musician?

A: He was in it for the money.

●

Q: Did you hear about the Polish musician who played weddings?

A: He was in it for the music.

●

A city man decides that he wants to go duck hunting. He buys all the necessary equipment, then one day he drives a couple of hours out of the city until he comes to an area of marshland that he has heard is good for finding ducks. He gets a motel room, puts on his thigh-high boots, grabs his rifle, and goes back to the marsh.

He stands in the water up to his knees all day long. He waits and waits for hours, but doesn't even *see* any ducks. When night falls he returns to the motel feeling very discouraged. The next morning he gets up at dawn and returns to the marsh. Once again, he stands all day out in the cold water and he still can't even *see* any ducks.

Finally around dusk, he is just about to give up when he looks up and sees one lone duck flying through the sky. Quickly he shoulders his rifle and takes aim. Blam! He shoots but misses. He keeps firing rounds, and missing, until he only has one bullet left. He sets his sights on the now faraway bird and shoots. Blam!

Much to his surprise and delight, he sees that he

has scored a direct hit. The man watches as the bird falls to the ground. With great effort, he hurriedly wades through the water until he gets to the dry land where the bird is lying dead on the ground. As he walks toward the duck, he notices that a man in overalls and big heavy boots is walking toward him.

As the hunter bends down to pick up the bird the other man says, "Now wait just a minute. That's my duck."

"No, it's not," says the hunter. "*I* shot it."

"I know you did," replies the other man, "but I am the farmer who owns the land here where the duck came down, so it's *my* duck."

This starts an argument between the two men that gets hotter and hotter, until the farmer interrupts and says, "OK, I can see that we're going to have to settle this in the way that men in these parts have settled arguments for generations."

"Oh, yeah?" says the hunter. "How is that?"

"Well," explains the farmer, "first I kick you in the balls, then you kick me in the balls, then I kick you again. Then you kick me, I kick you, you kick me, and we just keep going on like this. Whoever is left standing at the end gets to keep the duck."

The hunter thinks to himself, "Let's see. I spent $150 for the down vest, $200 for the waders, $300 for the rifle, $180 dollars for the motel room, and I told *everyone* that I was going to come back to the city with a duck. So I guess I've got to do it."

"All right," he grumbles to the farmer. "Let's get started."

"OK," says the farmer, rubbing his hands together. "Spread your legs."

The hunter assumes a wide stance and the farmer backs up about ten paces to get a good running start.

He comes at the hunter, building up speed, and when he gets right in front of him, the farmer plants his left foot, swings his right leg around in a circle three times, and then *boom*, kicks him hard with his heavy boot.

The man goes flying up ten feet in the air, then comes down on his back. He flops around on the ground for about five minutes with his face turning purple and bright red. After five minutes of this he lies motionless on the ground, choking and turning blue. Finally after another five minutes he manages to pull himself up onto his hands and knees, gasping for air. After five more minutes he staggers unsteadily to his feet and looks at the farmer. "OK," he rasps, barely able to get the words out, "it's my turn."

"You know," says the farmer, " :.. *take* the duck."

●

Q: What's the definition of an economic advisor?

A: Someone who wanted to go into accounting, but didn't have the personality.

●

A man goes to the doctor and says, "Doc, you just *gotta* help me."

"What seems to be the problem?" asks the physician.

"Well, Doc," explains the man, "I have this strange condition. You see, I'm always letting out these really loud farts. It's really embarrassing. They don't *smell* at all. But they're so loud that *everyone* hears them. I mean, I'll be out on a date with a beautiful woman, we'll be sitting in a really nice, romantic restaurant, and then all of a sudden one of these extremely loud farts will come out of me.

"Like I said, fortunately, these farts don't smell, but they make so much noise that it's very humiliating."

"Well," says the doctor reassuringly, "I think we'll be able to help you out without too much trouble. Why don't you just drop your pants and bend over, and I'll examine you."

The man follows the doctor's directions and right when the doctor crouches down and is looking at the man's exposed rear end, out comes one of the loudest farts the doctor has ever heard.

It makes a *boom* so loud that it shakes the walls of the office. When the echoes die down, the doctor shakes his head and stands up straight.

"Well," says the doctor, "it's obvious that we're going to have to operate."

"Oh, no!" says the man. Nervously he asks, "Are you going to have to operate on my asshole?"

"No," replies the doctor. "On your nose."

●

Q: **Why did the Mexican man throw the woman off the bridge?**

A: *He wanted tequila.*

●

Q: What's the difference between heaven and hell?

A: In heaven:

> the policemen are English,
>
> the cooks are French,
>
> the mechanics are German,
>
> the lovers are Italian,
>
> and the whole thing is run by the Swiss.

In hell:

> the policemen are German,
> the cooks are English,
> the mechanics are French,
> the lovers are Swiss,
> and the whole thing is run by the Italians.

●

Two friends who are struggling actors in New York City become taxi drivers to help support their artistic ambitions. After a couple of months of driving, one of the actors gets a part in a movie and is flown out to L.A. When the movie is released, it turns out to be a big hit and the actor goes on to become a big international movie star.

His friend, however, continues to drive a cab and keeps hoping for his big break. All the while, he closely follows his friend's career, sees all his films, and vicariously enjoys his success.

Ten years pass and one day the actor is in New York on a promotional tour and he hails a cab. As luck would have it, the driver turns out to be his old friend. They are very happy to see each other.

After spending a few minutes catching up, the cab driver says, "Lou, tell me something. We were in acting classes together for many years. We went to the same auditions and at that time we were fairly equal in our acting ability. Yet you went out to Hollywood and became a great movie star, and I'm still here, struggling in New York, driving a taxi.

"Lou, is there anything that you have learned over the years that you could tell me about the acting profession? Something that would help me become more like you, a successful actor?"

"Yes, there is," replies Lou, "and I can sum it up in one word."

"Really?" the cabbie says with excitement, "Just one word? What is it?"

"Sincerity," replies Lou.

"Sincerity?" the cabbie asks. "That's it?"

"Yep," says the actor, "Sincerity. Once you learn to fake that, you can do *anything*."

Q. What's the difference between L.A. and yo-gurt?

A: Yogurt has an active culture.

•

One day an actor telephones his agent. "Hello," he says, "is Sid there?"

The secretary who has answered the phone tells him, "Um, well, no. You see . . . a few days ago . . . Sid . . . passed away."

"Oh," says the actor. "Thank you." Then he hangs up.

Five minutes later the actor calls back. "Hello," he says, "is Sid there?"

The secretary replies, "I think you called before. You see, I'm afraid that Sid *died* a few days ago."

"Oh," says the actor. "Thank you." Then, once again, he hangs up.

Five more minutes go by, and then he phones again. "Hello," he says, "is Sid there?"

At this point the secretary explodes. "Look," she says angrily, "this is the third time you've called. I told you, *Sid is dead!* What do you keep calling for?"

"Well," says the actor, "it just sounds so good to hear you say it."

•

Q: How many movie studio executives does it take to change a light bulb?

A: "Does it have to be a light bulb?"

•

After a hard day making the rounds in L.A., an actor drives home to his house in the Hollywood Hills. As he pulls into his driveway, he is shocked to see that his house has burned to the ground. His wife and children are nowhere to be seen.

The actor bolts out of the car and runs to the next-door neighbor's house, and knocks frantically on the door. When the neighbor answers, the actor asks hysterically, "Do you know what happened to my house? Where is my family?"

"Oh, my God," cries the neighbor, "it was horrible! Your agent came over, ran inside your house, raped your wife, axed your children, and then torched the whole place."

The actor takes a step backward and stands there, stupefied. "My agent," he says in shocked disbelief, "came to my house?"

•

An agent out in Hollywood is talking to the devil. The devil says to the agent, "Look, I can make you richer, more famous, and more successful than any agent alive today. Actually, I can make you the greatest agent that has ever lived."

"Well," says the agent, "what do I have to do in return?"

The devil smiles. "Well, of course you have to give me your soul," he says, "but you also have to give me the souls of your children, the souls of your children's children, and, as a matter of fact, you have to give me the souls of all your descendants throughout eternity."

"Wait a minute," says the agent cautiously. "What's the catch?"

•

Q: What has four legs, is big, green, and furry, and if it fell out of a tree it would kill you?

A: A pool table.

●

A Japanese man walks into a bank in New York City, pushing a wheelbarrow full of yen. "I want to buy American dollars!" he says in a thick Japanese accent. "I want to buy American dollars!"

He is directed to the currency-exchange department, where it takes three men several hours to count all the Japanese money. When they finish, the bank officer hands the Japanese man a stack of U.S. currency, and says to him, "There you go, sir. That came out to eight thousand U.S. dollars."

The man smiles, bows politely, then leaves.

Two days later, the Japanese man enters the bank again, pushing another wheelbarrow full of yen. "I want to buy American dollars! I want to buy American dollars!"

Once more, he is directed to the currency exchange and after the men take several hours once again to count the money, the officer hands the man another stack of U.S. bills. He says, "Today that comes out to seven thousand five hundred dollars."

The Japanese man flies into a rage. "You're trying to cheat me!" he cries in broken English. "But you can't cheat me! I came in here two days ago with the same amount of yen and it came out to *eight* thousand dollars! I *know* how much it is worth!"

"Sir, you don't understand," the bank officer replies politely. "You see, the yen is just not valued as highly today on the world market as it was two days ago."

"You're trying to trick me!" shouts the man. "You think that because I'm Japanese I won't know the difference." At this point the man is shouting so loud that he is creating a scene in the bank. "You think that because I'm in a foreign country and don't speak perfect English, that you can take advantage of me!"

"That's not what it's about at all," says the banker, still trying to be patient. "It's about *fluctuations*."

The Japanese man points a shaking finger at the banker and screams, "No! Fluck you *Americans!*"

●

Q: **What is the difference between capitalism and communism?**

A: *Under capitalism, man exploits man, whereas under communism, it's the other way around.*

●

A guy goes into a sports bar with his dog under his arm. The bartender takes one look at the guy and says, "Hey! Get that dog outta here!"

"Wait a minute, sir," says the man. "*Please!* My dog is a really big Jets fan and my TV is busted. We can't watch the football game at home and my dog will go crazy if he misses it."

"Forget it!" answers the bartender. "The dog will start barking and he's liable to mess all over the place—"

"No! I *promise*," pleads the man. "My dog is really well-trained. I swear to you that he won't cause any trouble at all!"

"Well . . . " says the bartender, "all right. I guess

I'll let you stay. But at the first sign of any problem, you're both out of here.''

''Thanks, pal,'' says the man, ''thanks a lot! You won't regret this.''

He picks up his dog and quickly moves over to where the TV is showing the Jets game, which has already started. The guy sets his dog on the bar right in front of the television, and the dog's eyes remain fixed intently on the screen.

About ten minutes into the game, the Jets attempt to score a field goal. They kick the ball through the uprights and when the referee signals that the field goal was successful, the dog starts doing back flips on the bar. He then goes up and down the bar, giving everyone high-fives.

The bartender walks over to the dog owner and says, "Hey, buddy, that's quite a dog you have there! That was an amazing reaction. I've never seen anything like it. But tell me, if your dog goes that wild when they score a field goal, what does he do when they score a *touchdown?*"

"I don't know," replies the man. "I've only had the dog for five years."

●

Q: Did you hear about the new Chinese restaurant that has really hot, spicy food?

A: It's called Szechuan Fire.

●

A sweet potato arrives home and she is very excited. "Mommy," she shouts, "I'm going to get married!"

"That's wonderful!" says her mother. "Who is the lucky man?"

"Tom Brokaw," replies the happy sweet potato.

"Tom Brokaw?" Her mother exclaims. "Why, you can't marry *him.*"

"I can't?" asks the shocked sweet potato. "Why not?"

"Because, you are a sweet potato," explains the mother, "and he's just a commentator."

●

A termite walks into a bar and asks, "Where's the bar tender?"

●

A woman is sitting by the bedside of her dying husband. Suddenly the man takes her hand and says, "Martha, we've been married for fifty-five years, and before I go, there's something I need to get off of my conscience."

"Yes, dear," the woman gently replies, "What is it?"

"Before I tell you," says the man, gripping her hand tightly, "you must promise me that you will forgive me."

"Of course," says the woman.

"Say it," says the man, "Say 'I promise.' "

"Certainly dear," says the woman, "I promise I'll forgive you."

"Well," begins the man, "do you remember when we lived at the house on Hamilton Street?"

"Yes, dear," answers the woman, "we had some wonderful years there together."

"And," continues the man, "remember Rose, our next door neighbor?"

"One of my dearest, closest friends." reminisces the wife.

"Well," says the husband nervously, "I had an affair with her."

The wife's eyes widen in shock. "Max," she cries, "Rose? How could you—"

Max quickly interrupts, "Do you forgive me? Do you forgive me?"

The woman thinks for a moment, then, in slow measured tones, pointing a finger at Max, says, "Well ... OK ... BUT YOU'D BETTER DIE!"

Q: What's the difference between an oral thermometer and a rectal thermometer?

A: *The taste*.

●

When Moses came down from the mountain after talking with God, he was met by a crowd of people. They were overjoyed to see him, and they all gathered around to hear about his experience of talking with the supreme being. Moses was carrying in his arms the stone tablets with the commandments carved into them.

"How did it go?" the people asked.

"I have some good news and some bad news," answered the leader of the Israelites. "The good news is that I managed to whittle Him down to *ten*. The bad news is that adultery is still in."

●

An eighty-year-old woman goes to the doctor and finds out, much to her great surprise, that she is pregnant. She immediately calls her husband on the telephone. "You old coot," she says. "You got me pregnant."

The husband pauses for a moment, then asks, "Who is this?"

●

Three hookers are sitting around discussing the pet names that they call their boyfriends. One of them says, "Well, I call my boyfriend Coca-cola, because he's got the *real thing*, and I gets it whenever I wants it."

The second one chimes in, "Well, I call my boyfriend 7 Up, because he has *seven inches* and I gets it whenever I wants it."

They both turn to the third prostitute. "Well," they ask, "what do you call *your* man?"

The third prostitute smiles and replies:

"I calls him Courvoisier."

"*Courvoisier*?" says the first hooker. "Ain't that some fancy liquor?"

The third hooker just keeps grinning, nods her head, and slowly says, "Uh-huh."

•

Two Arabs and a Jewish man board a commercial airliner, and as it turns out they are all seated together in the same row. The Jewish man has the aisle seat and the Arabs have the two inside seats.

They all sit down and the Jewish man takes off his shoes, puts his feet up, and has just gotten comfortable when the Arab next to the window stands up.

"Excuse me," says the Arab, "but I'd like to go get myself a Coke."

Immediately the Jewish man replies, "Hey, I'd be *glad* to get you a Coke. Just sit back down, relax, and I'll have your Coke for you in a minute."

So off he goes to get the soda. While he is away, the Arab looks down and sees that the Jewish man has left his shoes on the floor. The Arab then leans over and spits into one of the shoes.

A moment later the Jewish man returns.

"Here is your Coke," he says kindly, handing it to the Arab. "I hope that you enjoy it."

The Jewish man sits down, puts his feet up, and has just gotten comfortable again when the Arab in the middle stands up. "Excuse me," says the second Arab, "but that Coke looked so good I just *have* to get one for myself."

"Hey," says the Jewish man, "I'd be glad to get one for *you,* too. Sit there, relax, and I'll be right back." And with a smile, he goes off to get the other Arab his Coke.

This time, the second Arab leans down and spits into the man's other shoe. When the Jewish man returns, he gives the Arab his Coke.

"There you go," he says, "and if you want another, please feel free to ask."

So the Jewish man sits down, puts his feet up once again, and finally gets comfortable. He then falls contentedly asleep.

A couple hours later, the airliner lands, and the three men start getting ready to deplane. The Jewish man puts on his shoes, and as soon as he stands up, he realizes exactly what has happened. He turns to the two Arabs next to him, and in a very exasperated voice says to them, "Oh, my God, when is this nonsense between us going to *end*? The spitting in the shoes . . . the pissing in the Cokes . . . "

●

Q: Did you hear about the new Jewish-American Princess horror movie?

A: It's called Debbie Does Dishes.

●

Q: Did you hear about the Jewish-American Princess porno movie?

A: It's called Debbie Does Nothing.

●

A priest and a rabbi who are very good friends coincidentally need to buy new cars at the same time, so they go shopping together. They visit all the car dealers, and both of them wind up choosing the same model and the same make of car.

They buy the two cars and are just about to drive them out of the dealership, when they decide that it might be a nice gesture for each of them to bless the other one's car.

So the priest goes over to the rabbi's car and sprinkles it with holy water. Then the rabbi goes over to the priest's car and cuts two inches off the tail pipe.

●

Did you hear about the dyslexic rabbi? He was walking around everywhere saying, "Yo!"

●

Q: How does a Jewish-American Princess change a light bulb?

A: *She says, "Daddy, I want a new apartment."*

●

Two men are hiking through the woods when they notice that a huge grizzly bear has begun following them. They can see by the way the animal is licking his chops that he is hungry. The bear keeps looking at them, and it soon becomes very obvious how he wants to satisfy his hunger.

The bear starts moving more quickly, and the two men begin walking faster and faster, trying to be as nonchalant as they can. Finally, one of the men can't take it any longer. He sits down on the ground, and quickly takes his sneakers out of his pack. He then begins to rapidly change from his hiking boots into his running shoes.

"Are you crazy?" says the other man. "You can't outrun a grizzly!"

"I know," says the man as he finishes tying his sneakers. "All I have to do is outrun *you*."

●

A philosopher walks into a bar and sits down. The bartender comes over to him and asks, "Would you like a drink?"

The philosopher says, "I think not," and disappears.

●

A six-year-old boy is watching a Western on television one evening. At a certain point in the show, he sees a cowboy walk up to a woman, rip the dress off her shoulder, and say to her, "I *want* what I *want* when I *want* it!" The boy switches off the TV, and sinks deep into thought.

The next day at school, the boy goes up to a little girl in his class and pulls her dress down off of her shoulder. He then says, "I *want* what I *want* when I *want* it."

The girl looks at him and says, "You'll *get* what I *got* when I *get* it."

•

Q: How can you tell when your house has been burglarized by gays?

A: *When you come home, you find that all your furniture has been tastefully rearranged.*

•

Late one night, two hookers are standing on their usual street corner when one of them says to the other, "How has your night been so far?"

"Kind of interesting," replies the second prostitute.

"Really?" says the first. "What happened?"

"Well," begins the woman, "earlier tonight a man came up to me here on the corner and asked if we could go back to the alley. I said, 'Sure'.

"When we got to that dark place behind the liquor store, the man asked me, 'How much would it cost to have sex with you?'

"I told him, 'A hundred bucks.'

" 'Gee, I don't have that much,' he said. So I told him, 'Well, I could give you a blow job for fifty.'

"He said, 'Golly, I don't have that much either.' So I was starting to get a little annoyed.

" 'Just how much *do* you have?' I asked. He dug down deep into his pocket, fished around, and then pulled out this crumpled-up twenty-dollar bill.

"I said, 'Twenty dollars, huh? Well, I suppose I could give you a hand job for twenty bucks.'

" 'Gosh,' he said, 'I don't know.'

"He just stood there thinking about it until I said, 'Well . . . ?'

"Finally, he said, 'Gee . . . uh . . . o.k.' So he unzipped his pants, and let me tell you, he pulled out the biggest tool I have ever seen in my entire life!"

"Wow!" says the first hooker. "What did you do?"

"What *could* I do?" replies the second hooker. "I loaned him eighty bucks."

• -

Q: You are in a room with a mass murderer, a terrorist, and a lawyer, and you have a gun with only two bullets in it. What do you do?

A: Shoot the lawyer twice.

•

A koala bear goes into a tavern and sits down at the bar. As he's having his beer, a woman comes up and sits down on the stool next to him. "Hello!" she says.

"G'day," says the koala.

"You're not from around here, are you?" asks the woman.

"No," replies the bear. "I'm from Australia."

"Well, you're kind of cute," says the woman, moving in closer to the little bear.

"You're not so bad yourself," replies the koala.

"How would you like to come up to my apartment?" asks the woman.

"Sounds great," says the bear, and off they go.

As soon as they get inside the door of the apartment, the koala bear rips the woman's clothes off and throws her on the bed. He then proceeds to go down on her. After about a half hour of this, the bear gets up and starts to walk out.

"Where are you going?" asks the woman.

"Back to the bar," answers the koala.

"You don't seem to understand," says the woman. "You see, I'm a prostitute."

"Prostitute?" says the bear. "What's that?"

"Here," says the woman, and tosses a dictionary at the koala bear. "Look it up."

The bear flips through the pages, then says, "Oh! Here it is."

"Now pay particular attention," says the hooker, "to the part of the definition where it says 'performs sexual favors in return for money.' "

"But," says the Australian animal, "I'm a koala bear."

"So what?" asks the woman. "What's a koala bear?"

"Look it up," says the koala, and tosses the dictionary back to the woman.

She pages through the book until she finds it. "Ah! Here it is," she says.

"Now pay particular attention," says the koala bear, "to the part of the definition where it says 'eats bushes and leaves.' "

•

Q: **What's the difference between a frog driving down the road in a car and a trombone player driving down the road in a car?**

A: *The frog might be driving to a gig.*

•

Two saxophone players happen to arrive on a street corner at the same exact time. Seeing each other's instrument cases, they look up and are startled to realize that they are long-lost friends.

"Richie! It's you!" exclaims one of the musicians.

"Eric!" says the other. "I can't believe it! I haven't seen you since we were together at the Berklee College of Music!"

"That was *ten years* ago," says Eric. "Wow! The time passes so quickly! Tell me, Richie, what have you been doing all this time?"

"Well," says Richie, "a few months after I got out of school, I wrote a song that was a big hit record."

"Really?" says Eric. "That's very hip. I'm surprised that I didn't hear a thing about that."

"Yeah, it was a real groove! Then," Richie continues, "I got called out to Hollywood to do a film score. I did it, and I wound up winning an Oscar!"

"Far out!" says Eric. "I can't believe that I didn't hear anything about that."

"Then," Richie goes on, "I put a band together and we did an album that made it to number one on the jazz charts."

"Gimme five, Richie," says Eric. After they slap skin, Eric says, "It's remarkable that I didn't hear anything about *that*, either."

Richie says, "Dig it! And while the album was still hot, the band went on The Tonight Show—*nationwide television!* But that night on the show there was a technical problem with the sound, and we couldn't hear each other. It was so bad that we couldn't play right, and we totally bombed."

"You know," says Richie, "I think I heard about that."

●

I was talking to a guy I know and he said, "Man, I sure wish I could screw Madonna again."

I was really surprised. "*You* screwed *Madonna?*" I asked.

"No," he said. "I wished I could screw her *yesterday*, too."

●

One day President Bush receives a call on his red telephone in the Oval Office. When he picks it up he hears a friendly voice on the line.

"George, this is Misha."

"Gorby!" replies Bush. "How are you?"

"I'm fine, George," answers Gorbachev, "but I need to ask a favor of you."

"Well, I'll help if I can," offers Bush. "What is it?"

"George, this whole AIDS thing has gotten us pretty worried over here," Gorbachev confides. "We need ten million more condoms right away, but our manufacturers just can't handle the entire load. Do you think that you could rush me a shipment of seven million condoms next week?"

"I'll make some calls and see what I can do," replies President Bush.

"Just one more favor, George," says Gorbachev. "Do you think they could make the condoms sixteen inches long?"

"Gee, I'll do my best and get back to you right away," says Bush.

They hang up and the president immediately calls the largest condom manufacturer in the United States. "Hello, this is President Bush," he says.

The manufacturer is astonished. "Mr. President! What an honor to have you call! Is there anything that I can do for you?"

"Well, my friend, there is," begins Bush. "I need to ask you for a favor."

"Anything!" says the manufacturer.

"I just got a call from Mikhail Gorbachev in Russia. The AIDS situation has gotten them pretty scared over there, and they need some more condoms. Could you ship out an order of seven million condoms to them next week?"

"Of course, Mr. President," says the manufacturer. "It will require running our factory twenty-four hours a day, but I am only too happy to oblige."

"Thank you, sir," replies President Bush. "However, I have another favor to ask of you."

"No problem," says the manufacturer. "What is it?"

"I would like," says Bush, "for you to make the condoms sixteen inches long. Could you do that?"

The manufacturer thinks for a moment, then replies, "Well, it will involve retooling some of our machines, but for *you*, Mr. President, I am very happy to do anything that I can."

"There's just one more favor I'd like to ask of you," says the president. "On these seven million sixteen-inch condoms I would like for you to stamp 'Made in U.S.A. - MEDIUM.' "

Q: What's the difference between a lawyer and a vulture?

A: Frequent-flier miles.

•

A drunk is driving through the city and his car is weaving violently all over the road. An Irish cop soon pulls him over. "So," says the cop to the driver, "where have *you* been?"

"I been to the pub," slurs the drunk.

"Well," says the cop, "it looks like you've had quite a few."

"I did all right," smiles the drunk.

"Did you know," says the cop, standing up straight and folding his arms, "that a few intersections back, your *wife* fell out of your car?"

"Oh, thank heavens," sighs the drunk. "For a minute there, I thought I'd gone deaf."

•

Reagan dies and goes to heaven. He is standing at the pearly gates and Saint Peter welcomes him. "Your name, please?" asks the saint.

"Ronald Reagan," comes the reply.

"Do you have any proof?" asks Saint Peter.

"Proof? What do you mean, proof?" says the Californian. "I'm Ronald Reagan! Ex-president of the United States! C'mon! Let me into heaven!"

"You look sort of familiar," says Saint Peter, "but I need some proof."

Reagan becomes angry. "I'm President Reagan!" he shouts. "Let me into heaven!"

"I can't let you in without proof," Saint Peter answers.

"Well, what kind of proof are you talking about?" asks the frustrated Ronnie.

"For instance," recalls Saint Peter, "I remember when Mozart arrived, we gave him a piano. In ten minutes he had written a beautiful concerto. Well, it was obviously Mozart, so we let him into heaven.

"When Picasso came here," continues Saint Peter, "we gave him a brush, some oil paint, and a canvas and right away he painted us a beautiful picture. We immediately knew it was Picasso and we let him right into heaven."

Reagan looks at Saint Peter and says, "Mozart and Picasso? Who are they?"

Saint Peter jerks his thumb over his shoulder and replies, "You're Reagan, all right. Come on in."

•

Q: **Why do you bury lawyers 1,000 feet under the ground?**

A: *Because deep down, they're probably all right.*

•

Q: **How do you get an electric-guitar player to turn down the volume on his amplifier?**

A: *Put a chart in front of him.*

•

The first manned space voyage goes to Mars. When the astronauts finally touch down on the surface of the red planet, they emerge from the landing module and look around at the unusual landscape. They climb down the ladder and as soon as they set foot on the strange planet, they see an odd-looking vehicle driving right toward them. It quickly pulls up to within ten feet of where the astronauts are standing, and then stops.

The door opens and a Martian gets out. "Where are you from?" asks the Martian, in perfect English.

One of the astronauts draws himself up to his full height and proudly says, "We're from Earth."

"Oh, wow!" says the Martian. "You're from Earth! Do you know a guy named—"

•

A flasher was thinking of retiring, but he decided to stick it out for another year.

●

Q: What's the worst thing about being an atheist?

A: *When you're getting a blow job, you've got no one to talk to.*

●

Two Irish women are working in the garden together. One of them, Molly, suddenly pulls a carrot out of the ground. "Oh, my, Kathleen," she says, "this carrot really reminds me of Seamus."

"Oh, *does* it now?" asks Kathleen with a slight chuckle. "And what is it about this carrot that reminds you of Seamus? Is it the length, maybe?"

"No, no," says Molly, "it's not the length of it that reminds me of Seamus."

"Well, then," Kathleen inquires, flushing a bit, "is it maybe the breadth that reminds you of Seamus?"

"No," answers Molly, "it's not the breadth that reminds me of him, either."

"Good Lord," asks Kathleen, "what exactly *is* it about that carrot then that reminds you so much of Seamus?"

"Well," replies Molly, "it's the dirt all over it."

●

Q: What's the difference between an Italian-American Princess and a Jewish-American Princess?

A: *With an Italian-American Princess, the jewels are fake and the orgasms are real.*

●

Q: What's the difference between a trampoline and a violin?

A: *You have to take off your shoes before you jump on a trampoline.*

●

A Polish man is sitting in a restaurant when all of a sudden a woman at the table next to him begins to choke on her food. It has become lodged in her throat and she can't breathe at all. The people at her table all start to panic and don't know what to do, and the woman is beginning to turn blue.

Suddenly the Polish man leaps from his chair, runs over to the woman, pulls up her dress, yanks down her underwear, and starts running his tongue all over her bare ass. The woman is so shocked by this that she swallows really hard and her food goes right down.

The woman starts breathing again, and the people at her table surround the Polish man. "You saved her!" they cry with joy. "You saved her life! How did you know so quickly what to do?" they ask.

"Aw," says the Polish guy, casually, "that heinie-lick maneuver works every time."

●

Q: What's brown and sounds like a bell?

A: *Dung.*

●

Two junkies are sitting around shooting up. Suddenly, one of the addicts says to the other, "Hey, man, can I borrow your needle?"

"Sure," the second one replies, "but I have to warn you. I've got AIDS."

"Hey, no problem," says the first junkie. "I'm wearing a condom!"

●

Two Southern belles are talking, and one of them has just returned from a trip up to New York City. "Do you know," she tells her friend confidentially, "that up there in New York, they have *men* who kiss *men?*"

"Mercy me!" replies the friend. "What do they call people like that?"

"Well," says the traveler, "they call those people *homosexuals*. And do you know, that up there in New York they have *women* who kiss *women?*"

"Oh, my Lord," cries the other woman, totally shocked. "What on earth do they call people like *that?*"

"Well," says the first woman, "they call those people *lesbians*. And . . . do you know that up there in New York they have *men* who kiss women down *there?*"

"Heavens to Betsy!" gasps the incredulous friend. "I don't believe it! Why, what on earth do they call people like *that?*"

"Well," says the first woman, "once I regained my composure, I called him *precious*."

●

Q: What's the difference between a Jewish-American Princess and a pit bull?

A: Lip gloss.

●

Two women are walking through the woods when suddenly they hear a voice say, "Ladies! Ladies!" They look around but don't see anyone. Then they hear it again. "Ladies! Ladies! Down here!'' They look down and see a small pond with a frog sitting on a lily pad.

"Is that you?" one of the ladies asks the frog.

"Yes," is the frog's reply.

The two women are in shock. "How can you talk to us?" They ask. "You're a frog."

"I got turned into a frog by a wicked witch," explains the frog. "I'm really a fantastic jazz saxophone player."

"Really?" say the women. "Is that true?"

"Yes," answers the frog, "and all it will take is one kiss from either of you, and I will immediately change back into a fantastic jazz saxophone player."

Right away, one of the women gets down on her knees, reaches across the pond to the lily pad and gently picks up the frog. She stands up and quickly puts the frog in her pocket and starts to walk away.

Her startled friend says, "Hey, wait a minute! Where are you going? He said that if you kiss him, he'll turn into a fantastic jazz saxophone player!"

"What are you, crazy?" says the other woman. "I can make a *lot* more money with a talking frog than I can with a fantastic jazz saxophone player."

●

Two employees are talking. One of them asks the other, "How long have you been working here?"

The other one replies, "Since they threatened to fire me."

●

Three Frenchmen and an American woman are having dinner together. At one point during the conversation, the term savoir faire is used. The American woman says, "Excuse me, gentlemen, but I don't know what that means. What is the definition of 'savoir faire'?"

"Ah," says one of the Frenchmen, "it does not translate directly into English, but I think I can give you a *feeling* for what 'savoir faire' means.

"For example," he continues, "suppose a man comes home unexpectedly from a long business trip. He goes upstairs to the bedroom, opens the door, and finds his wife in bed with another man. He says, 'Oh, excuse me.' *That*, my friend, is savoir faire."

The second Frenchman cuts in, "Pardon me, please, but that is not really the *true* meaning of savoir faire. It is very cool, I admit, but it is not savoir faire. *Real* savoir faire is when a man comes home unexpectedly from a long business trip, goes upstairs to the bedroom, opens the door, and finds his wife in bed with another man. The husband says, 'Oh, excuse me. Please continue.' Now *that* is savoir faire."

The third Frenchman says, "That, I must admit, is very close to an accurate definition of savoir faire, but it is not quite right. Real, true savoir faire is when a man comes home unexpectedly from a long business trip, goes upstairs to the bedroom, opens the door, and finds his wife in bed with another man. The husband says, 'Oh, excuse me. Please continue.' If the man *continues*, THAT is savoir faire."

•

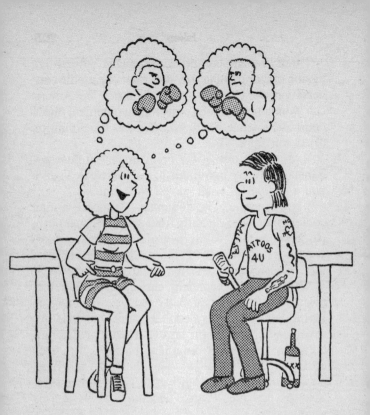

A woman walks into a tattoo parlor. She goes up to the tattoo artist and says to him, "I love boxing. I think it's the greatest sport ever invented by mankind. I watch it all the time, read all about it, and I want you to do a job for me."

"Sure," says the tattoo artist. "What would you like?"

The woman explains, "I want two tattoos, one on each thigh. On my right thigh, I want a portrait of Muhammed Ali, and on my left thigh, a portrait of Mike Tyson. These are my two favorite boxers of all time."

"Well," says the artist somewhat hesitantly, "you're talking about a lot of work. That will cost a lot of money."

"Money is no object," says the woman. "I don't care how much it costs. Just give me something to knock me out while you do the job."

"All right," agrees the tattoo artist. He gives the woman a bottle and she drinks it until she passes out.

The artist begins, and he gets completely absorbed in his work, losing all track of time. Nine hours later, he leans back to view his handiwork and he realizes that this is his masterpiece.

He is extremely proud as he excitedly wakes up the woman. "Look! Look!" he says.

The woman wakes up, looks down at her thighs, and asks, "What's this?"

"What do you mean, 'What's this?'" says the shocked tattoo artist. "It's the two tattoos you wanted!"

"But—but ... " stammers the woman. "It doesn't look anything like them."

"Are you kidding me?" says the incredulous tattoo artist. "It looks *exactly* like them!"

"No, it *doesn't*," says the woman. She motions back and forth between her thighs and whines, "I can't even tell which one is supposed to be which!"

"It's Ali on the *right*, Tyson on the *left*, just like you wanted," says the tattoo artist.

"This is just terrible!" cries the woman. "And now I have to live with this for the rest of my life!" She gets up and starts to leave.

The tattoo artist stops her. "Wait a minute, lady," he says. "I did a lot of work for you. You owe me some money."

At this, the woman becomes furious. "I'm not paying for this! You did a lousy job!"

"I did *not*," yells the tattoo artist. "I did a *great* job. It looks *just* like them."

"No, it doesn't," says the woman, and she bursts out of the tattoo parlor.

The man chases her out onto the street, and just then a bum happens to be walking by. The tattoo artist runs up to the woman, pulls up her dress, and shouts to the bum, "Who are these boxing greats?"

The bum staggers a moment, then drunkenly slurs, "I'm not sure about the guy on the right. The guy on the left, I don't know." Suddenly the bum brightens. "The guy in the middle, though," he says, "is definitely *Don King!*"

●

A very shy man has been dating a woman for several months and has only gotten up the nerve to kiss her once or twice. One night, as he is driving her home he decides to himself, "Tonight's the night I'm going to do it."

When they get to her house, he pulls the car right up in front and turns off the engine. Suddenly, he unzips his pants, grabs the woman's hand, and puts it right onto his penis.

"That's disgusting!" cries the woman. She gets out of the car, slams the door shut, and walks up the sidewalk to the house. As she gets up onto her front porch, she turns around and says to the man, "I only have two words to say to you: GOOD NIGHT!"

"I have only two words to say to *you*," replies the man in the car. "LET GO!"

●

Q: Why is wonton soup a Jewish-American Princess's favorite soup?

A: Because it's "not now" spelled backward.

●

A black man dies and goes to heaven. When he reaches the pearly gates he is met by Saint Peter.

"Welcome," says the saint. "You are about to enter the Kingdom of Heaven, but before I can let you in, I have to ask you just one question. What is the most magnificently stupendous thing that you ever did?"

"Oh, that's easy," replies the black man. "During the Alabama-Mississippi football game, underneath the stands, I boffed the granddaughter of the Grand Dragon of the KKK."

"Wow! That really is amazing!" exclaims Saint Peter. "Exactly when did you do that?"

"Oh," says the black man, "about five minutes ago."

●

A man goes to the doctor, "Doc," he says, "every time I sneeze I get an orgasm!"

"My goodness," replies the doctor. "What are you taking for it?"

The man says, "Pepper."

●

It is the 18th century and the King of England decides to go elk hunting. He gathers his entourage and they all head out on horseback into the English countryside. At the king's side is his First Man, carrying the king's trusty rifle.

They are riding through the woods, looking for game, when suddenly a man jumps out from behind a tree, waving his hands over his head. "DON'T SHOOT!" He cries, "DON'T SHOOT! I'M NOT AN ELK! I'M NOT AN ELK!"

The king immediately stops his horse and says to his First Man, "My rifle please." As the first man is loading the king's rifle, the man, waving his arms over his head, shouts again, "Don't shoot! I'm not an elk! I'm not an elk!"

The First Man hands the king his rifle and the king takes careful aim. Blam! He shoots the man dead.

The entire entourage sits in stunned silence, shocked at what has just occurred. Only the First Man, however, dares to speak. "Begging your pardon, sir," he says to the king, "but why did you shoot that man? After all, he was shouting, 'Don't shoot, I'm not an elk, I'm not an elk.' "

"Oh, my lord, this is tragic," says the king, suddenly crestfallen. "This is just terrible. I thought he was saying 'I *am* an elk.' "

●

A woman goes into a drugstore, in this enlightened day and age, and boldly says to the clerk, "I'D LIKE A BOX OF CONDOMS!"

Then she shields her mouth with her hand and whispers, " . . . and a pack of cigarettes."

●

Q: Gorbachev has a long one. Bush has a short one. Madonna doesn't have one. The Pope doesn't use his. What is it?

A: *A last name.*

●

Q: What's the difference between a woman with PMS and a terrorist?

A: *You can negotiate with a terrorist.*

●

AFTERWORD

Before I finish, I would like to leave you with one final thought, best expressed through an incident that happened to me some time ago.

I was playing drums for a band at a wedding one Saturday afternoon. During one of our breaks, the musicians were sitting at the table that had been set aside for the band and photographers, and we spontaneously began to tell jokes.

We happened to get into telling a string of Polish jokes and we were enjoying ourselves immensely until one of the guests, an older man, got up from his table which was situated (unfortunately) right next to ours. He came directly over to me.

"I heard those jokes you were telling," he said angrily, "and *I'm* Polish. Those jokes were extremely offensive to me."

I apologized, and tried to explain that the jokes were told only in fun, and that we had no intention of making anyone feel uncomfortable. I also said that we would stop right away, but the man wouldn't let it drop.

He started raising his voice and was beginning to disturb people at the other tables. I tried to calm him down, but he seemed to be losing control of himself. It was starting to become very embarrassing, but I was totally unprepared for what happened next.

The man pulled a razor on me.

I was shocked, and everyone else at our table just sat there staring in disbelief as this man was going over the edge of sanity. I was hoping he wouldn't go too far, when he suddenly started to actually threaten me with the razor.

In the end, though, it all turned out all right, because he couldn't find any place to plug it in.

Watch out for those suck-in jokes!

Enjoy!

The Best in Biographies from Avon Books

IT'S ALWAYS SOMETHING
by Gilda Radner   71072-2/$5.95 US/$6.95 Can

JACK NICHOLSON: THE UNAUTHORIZED BIOGRAPHY *by Barbara and Scott Siegel*
                         76341-9/$4.50 US/$5.50 Can

ICE BY ICE
by Vanilla Ice   76594-2/$3.95 US/$4.95 Can

CARY GRANT: THE LONELY HEART
by Charles Higham and Roy Moseley
                         71099-9/$5.99 US/$6.99 Can

I, TINA
by Tina Turner with Kurt Loder
                         70097-2/$4.95 US/$5.95 Can

ONE MORE TIME
by Carol Burnett   70449-8/$4.95 US/$5.95 Can

PATTY HEARST: HER OWN STORY
by Patricia Campbell Hearst with Alvin Moscow
                         70651-2/$4.50 US/$5.95 Can

PICASSO: CREATOR AND DESTROYER
by Arianna Stassinopoulos Huffington
                         70755-1/$4.95 US/$5.95 Can